Christ-
No More, No Less

Christ-
No More, No Less

*How to be a Christian in
a Postmodern World*

Milton Jones

with Michael Hall

NEW LEAF BOOKS

Orange, California

ISBN 0-9700836-2-9

Printed in the United States of America

10 9 8 7 6 5 4 3 2   08 07 06 05 04 03 02

For current information about all releases from New Leaf Books call toll free 1-877-634-6004 or write New Leaf Books, 12542 S. Fairmont, Orange, CA 92869.

To Barbie

My wife, my love, my friend.

You are truly a song in the night.

Happy 25th Anniversary!

Table of Contents

Preface

My hair was growing longer and longer. I wasn't exactly sure why, but I knew it was important. Hemlines were rising. Music was getting louder. And the whole world was watching. I knew things would never be the same. Not for me. Not for my world.

"The times they are a-changin'," Bob Dylan sang. No words could have been more true. It was the 60s. I was a student. I didn't know what was happening in my world, but I knew it was happening.

A war was raging, but I couldn't understand it. I loved my country but didn't like what I was seeing. There were a lot of things I didn't like. But things were changing. My professor told me that the only constant was change. I just didn't know what it would look like when it all changed.

Then I changed. And I got more hopeful about my world. I left the radical thoughts of the 60s and became a business major. But that wasn't enough. After becoming a fully devoted disciple of Jesus, I decided to give my life to ministry. And I became a campus minister at the University of Washington.

In 1979 I caught up with Dylan again. It was at the Paramount Theatre in Seattle. His latest album had just been released. And I couldn't wait to connect with Dylan to see how he had changed. Wow, had he ever changed. Every song that night was religious. He was now singing about Jesus. He sang, "It may be the devil or it may be the Lord, but you're gonna have to serve somebody!" It had taken awhile, but it looked like things had changed. His album was called "Slow Train Coming." Was this the end of the line?

But something happened in the 90s. I couldn't quite put my finger on it, but things had changed more than ever. Harold Shank and Chris Altrock invited me to Memphis to speak on current cultural changes. But I had to turn them down because I just wasn't able to define what was happening. Then I went to a seminar hosted by Ivy Jungle, and they explained to me that our world was now postmodern. If only I knew what that meant. Reading books on postmodernism only confused me more. They were the most difficult reading matter I had ever encountered.

Fortunately I got to listen to Bob Dylan one more time. He explained it. As we had entered the new millennium, Dylan was no longer singing, "The times they are a-changin'." Now he was singing, "People are crazy and times are strange. . . I used to care, but things have changed." And near the end he sings, "All the truth in the world adds up to one big lie." That's postmodernism.

How did he get there? I wish it was just a song. But it doesn't take a rocket scientist or a rock musician to know that the world has changed. And I'm not sure I like it.

What changed? How do we understand it? And what do we do?

That's what this book is all about. I think Christians need to understand postmodernism to have an effective witness in this world. But I'm very realistic about it. I don't think the average guy in the pew is going to wade through all the philosophical verbiage to get an answer. Decades ago Fritz Ridenour wrote some books that examined the philosophy of his age in a simple manner and provided biblical answers from the context of a New Testament book. I wanted to do the same thing with postmodernism. This won't be the deepest book on postmodernism. In fact, the goal is just the opposite. There are better and more comprehensive works out there, but this one hopes to be more like "Postmodernism for Dummies."

Richard Middleton and Brian Walsh have written the best analysis of this philosophy that I have read. I wanted to take some of their ideas to a more general audience and then make some unique New Testament applications.

Whenever a major problem exists, I believe the Bible will address it, at least in principle. I believe that the problem of postmodernism is best addressed in the book of Colossians. A bad philosophy had entered the culture of Colossae. And it had even penetrated the life of the church. The Apostle Paul wrote to this church and told them how to find an answer to the philosophy of their age. He taught them that the answer is found in "Christ—No More, No Less." Many things have changed over the last 2000 years. I don't think this is one of them.

Milton Jones
August 2000

Acknowledgements

My thanks goes out to the Northwest Church of Christ in Seattle for their amazing patience. They have now listened to me preach for 23 years. This book started out as a series of Sunday morning sermons at Northwest. The congregation gave me tremendous encouragement and urged me to do more with the series. Every week Jack Riehl told me to write a book.

When I didn't, Michael Hall, my colleague and an attorney at Puget Sound Christian College, took the tapes and put them in manuscript form. He was determined that this series would become a book even if I wasn't.

Leonard Allen, who had created New Leaf Books to bring an awareness of postmodern thought and culture to Christians, found out about my project from Chris Seidman. Leonard encouraged and motivated me to finish the course. As a result, I took the manuscript and completed the book.

Thank you Kent Landrum and Ann McMurray for always finding illustrations and pictures when they were needed. And thanks to Leonard for editing this book over and over again. If it communicates well he deserves credit.

I also want to thank several of my friends who helped me think through these philosophical ideas. Among them are Scott Sager, Ken Hensley, Jeff Berryman, Joel Solliday, Mark Krause and Jeffrey Crouch.

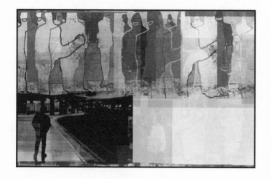

Jesus Is the Answer!

"Jesus is the Answer!" You could see the sign from nearly any-place traveling through Tacoma on Interstate 5. The message was a great alternative to the myriads of advertising monoliths looming over the freeway fastlanes. But I can imagine someone catching a fleeting glimpse of the message and asking, "If Jesus is the answer, then what is the question?"

As we came to the last decade of the twentieth century, it was obvious that the world was changing drastically. The pat answers that had been given for hundreds of years to the big questions of our exis-tence were no longer being heard. Did Christians still really have an answer? And if they did, how did it relate to what was really on everyone's mind?

What is Postmodernism?

As the world changed, a new name emerged. Our Western world is now being called "postmodern." When did it happen? The current debate about postmodernism has yet to determine just when this new cultural era actually started. Some would say it began with the fall of the Berlin Wall. Others place its beginnings much earlier. The answer will probably depend on who writes the history books.

Even though postmodernism is difficult to define, it is very much in vogue today. A contemporary theologian described postmodernism as "the intellectual velcro dragged across culture which can be used to characterize almost anything one approves or disapproves."[1] As Umberto Eco, author of *The Name of the Rose*, said, "I have the impression that it [postmodernism] is applied today to anything the users of the term happen to like."[2]

It may be helpful to compare postmodernism with other historical periods to make the concept easier to grasp. If we compare and contrast the Medieval Period, the Modern Period and the Postmodern Period, the analysis would look something like the following:

	Medieval	Modern	Postmodern
How People Communicate	Orally	Printing Press	Hypertext
How the World is Known	World can't be known; it is mysterious	World is knowable through science	Science & mysticism combined
Who's In Charge	God writes the story	Man writes the story	No story

From the chart it is easy to see how times have drastically changed. In communication the world has moved from orality to books to computers. In regard to knowledge we have gone from mystery to science to someplace in between. In existential understanding we have regressed from a divine plan to a self-made human plan to a non-existent plan. In the most important areas of life our current postmodern culture no longer resembles the past.

Though the postmodern cultural shift has come about as a result of hundreds of changes in this modern culture, there are essentially four pivotal transitions that have distinctively shaped this new philosophical outlook.[3] These movements can be called "The Four Posts of Postmodernism."

The Four Posts of Postmodernism

1. The Fall of the West

The first "post" of postmodernism focuses on what many call the "Fall of the West." At one point in history, Western philosophy basically took over the Western world. During this unique period of development, it was assumed that the pursuit of capitalism, urbanization, technology, telecommunications, and Western culture would continue indefinitely simply because it was said to be "better."

However, in our postmodern society this Western philosophy of development is now being widely questioned. Is it really better? In art we seem to be lost in the realm of abstraction. Has art truly become better? Unless you are one of a few art aficionados the answer would be negative. Our democratic political theory is being scrutinized more than ever. Are politics in our country really better than they used to be? No one seems to be saying that on their way to the polls. How about religion? Even Western religion is being widely critiqued for its long and profound secular drift. Marketing strategies now appear more important than theology as we have witnessed the emergence of the megachurch. Is this better?

Not very long ago we thought that with the passage of time everyone would adopt the values of our Western society. Not anymore. Something happened in the 1990s. The West lost its worldwide appeal.

How does this affect Christianity? Since Christianity has been seen as a Western religion, it has shared to some degree in the reign of the West. But now, with Western influence waning, there is a trend to rewrite history without the dominance of the Western rule.

For example, the role of Columbus in the history of the Americas is now being seen as less important and certainly less positive than it was depicted in the past. Because the Bible has been so tied to Western culture, it is also falling from its place of authority and favor.

2. The Fall of the Accepted

The next post of postmodernism is the "Fall of the Accepted" or the "legitimization crisis." The social mores of the past which were once accepted as authoritative are now being called into question. For instance, the traditional sexual values of the Judeo-Christian faith have been considered legitimate for several thousand years. Chastity before marriage was accepted as a given. Even if reality often fell short of the ideal, the traditional standard was accepted as having real value to society. Now it would seem that sexual activity before marriage, having children outside of marriage, living together, and even homosexuality are so common that they are being given legitimacy.

There is a moral crisis in postmodern society focused on the legitimacy of belief itself. With no universally held values, there is no way for any of us to say with authority that anything is legitimate. Therefore, we end up with a pluralism of values causing our society to fragment into special interest groups.

This same crisis of legitimacy can be seen in the Christian faith. Without universally held values, even among believers who differ in minor areas of doctrine or philosophy, Christians cannot present a universal message to the postmodern world.

3. The Fall of Intellectual Control

The third "post" of postmodernism is the "Fall of Intellectual Control" or the decline of the intellectual marketplace. In the not-so-distant past, parents controlled their children, teachers controlled their students, clergy controlled their congregations, and politicians controlled their citizenry. This control was maintained through "knowledge." Knowledge was power. The dissemination of knowledge was carefully controlled. Today, however, with the explosive advancement of technology, it has become increasingly difficult for the intellectual and political elite to limit access to cultural, political or even religious knowledge.

A few decades ago, for example, church members basically knew only what was happening in their particular church or at least in their particular movement or denomination. Biblical understanding and even how church worked was pretty well limited to the information that came from the minister. Things have changed. With television, contemporary Christian music, and mass gatherings like Promise Keepers, church members know what else is out there. The local minister is only one small voice in the church members' religious input.

Nowhere has this been more evident than in the area of music. For hundreds of years church music was what you heard at church. Your particular repertoire was limited to your own congregation or annual gatherings with other churches that were just like yours. Now most Christians know what is happening in other churches, and they are bringing the music they prefer home with them. Debates over worship teams, praise choruses, keyboards, drums and guitars are happening in nearly every congregation because local leadership no longer controls knowledge of the options.

4. The Fall of Texts

The fourth major "post" of postmodernism is "The Fall of Texts" or what is known as "Deconstruction." Deconstruction is the process of peeling apart a text like you would peel an onion. The text is not accepted as a whole, but rather dissected or torn apart.

Our current legal process is a good example of deconstruction. Justice does not seem to mean much anymore. By allowing detailed defenses aimed at nit-picking and twisting reality, the judicial process has become a megalith which is crumbling under its own weight. Even the recent attempts of our government to impeach President Clinton highlight the fall of the written word.

The interpretation of the President's testimony under oath reached the height of deconstruction when it seemed that any phrase or statement could be redefined to mean whatever the moment demanded. The trial demonstrated well that the written word has lost its universal meaning.

The critical problem with deconstruction is that nothing has a once-for-all meaning. This has shown itself to be a major problem with our national laws and even the Constitution itself. But for Christians the same problem exists with sacred texts. In the postmodern view, the meanings of documents evolve over time. This may not be a huge problem for some texts, but when it comes to the Bible, a critical dilemma occurs. Christians claim that the Bible is timeless truth from God; yet the major philosophy of our time dictates that no text is timeless and firm in its meaning.

How Can You Be a Christian in a Postmodern World?

So how do we fit Christianity into a postmodern world? It seems like a difficult question. And the sad answer to this perplexing question is that Christianity does not fit into the major posts of postmodernism. And yet churches everywhere are trying to adapt Christianity to the postmodern world. Many churches are taking more of an Eastern approach to religion by emphasizing an inner subjectivism and allowing for the validity of all religions. Others are changing or softening their core beliefs. Congregations are giving in to the intellectual marketplace where whatever is popular becomes the rule of thumb for the church. Many are proclaiming a message with no universal truths. The new trend is to create a church that is more pleasing to people of the postmodern mind, while avoiding those who do not fit into the postmodern philosophy.

In the postmodern world, Christianity must be seen as distinctive and not something that can be changed to fit an ever-changing mold. Indeed, Christianity and postmodernism, in many of their foundational tenets, are mutually exclusive. We cannot put

God into a postmodern box. Already some philosophers are saying that postmodernism is bankrupt. Already they are in search of
the next worldview. If this is the case, why would Christians even
try to be postmodern?

The pressing question is how to present Christianity as a viable
alternative in today's postmodern society. At this juncture, some
might advocate a return to modernism. However, that period of history did not suit Christians well either. Modernism itself created many
of the problems in churches today. Unable to differentiate properly
between what was rooted in Scripture and what was rooted in modernism, churches became frozen by hermeneutical disagreements.
Further, modernism created a religion without the mystery of God.
In modern churches intellect reigned supreme. But ultimately,
though it took a couple of centuries, we found out that a modern
church didn't work any better than a modern world.

Others might propose that we turn again to the premodern
world. Gabriel Moran asked an intriguing question: "Is the postmodern world a return to the premodern world?" In other words,
is the postmodern world more like the biblical world than was the
modern world?

If this is true, we may find particular help in the Scriptures for
the philosophical confusion we are facing today. Perhaps no biblical book addresses cultural chaos better than the book of
Colossians, for the Colossian church had been taken over by a
group of intellectuals who had decided to rewrite the Gospel to suit
their own philosophical ideas.

Colossians--Help for a Church in Cultural Chaos

Colossians is difficult to understand because of the particular problems that existed at the time. Some scholars say the problem was
a type of gnosticism. However, no known style of gnosticism exactly fits all the characteristics that were apparent in first-century
Colossae at that time. Their problem is usually called the
"Colossian heresy." Perhaps there was a particular brand of

heresy, but let's define the problem exactly the way Paul defined it. He called it "a philosophy." It was a pseudo-religious philosophy which had permeated the culture and had also entered the church causing an emphasis on some very questionable doctrine. Paul says, "See to it that no one takes you captive through hollow and deceptive philosophy, which depends on human tradition and the basic principles of this world rather than on Christ" (Col. 2:8).

Isn't this still our problem today? In our analysis of postmodernism thus far, wouldn't a "hollow and deceptive philosophy" work pretty well as a description of it? Is there any hope for us in a postmodern world? Do hollow and deceptive philosophies always win the day? In his day Paul was very optimistic that, with God's help, things could change at Colossae. As we continue our critique of postmodernism, we are going to look closely at Paul's advice to the church at Colossae, a church that was also struggling with a philosophy that contradicted much of their faith.

1 Paul, an apostle of Christ Jesus by the will of God, and Timothy our brother,

2 To the holy and faithful brothers in Christ at Colossae: Grace and peace to you from God our Father.

3 We always thank God, the Father of our Lord Jesus Christ, when we pray for you,

4 because we have heard of your faith in Christ Jesus and of the love you have for all the saints—

5 the faith and love that spring from the hope that is stored up for you in heaven and that you have already heard about in the word of truth, the gospel

6 that has come to you. All over the world this gospel is bearing fruit and growing, just as it has been doing among you since the day you heard it and understood God's grace in all its truth.

7 You learned it from Epaphras, our dear fellow-servant, who is a faithful minister of Christ on our behalf,

8 and who also told us of your love in the Spirit.

9 For this reason, since the day we heard about you, we have not stopped praying for you and asking God to fill you with the knowledge of his will through all spiritual wisdom and understanding.

10 And we pray this in order that you may live a life worthy of the Lord and may please him in every way: bearing fruit in every good work, growing in the knowledge of God,

11 being strengthened with all power according to his glorious might so that you may have great endurance and patience, and joyfully

12 giving thanks to the Father, who has qualified you to share in the inheritance of the saints in the kingdom of light.

13 For he has rescued us from the dominion of darkness and brought us into the kingdom of the Son he loves,

14 in whom we have redemption, the forgiveness of sins.
(Colossians 1:1-14)

Did you notice Paul's attitude in these verses? He honestly thinks that the negative issues in the Colossian church can be overcome. Wouldn't he also think that the power of the gospel is superior to the philosophical pull of postmodernism today? How important it is for Christians in our age not to give in to defeat on the front-line of philosophical challenges! The church will find an answer today when we too are "asking God to fill [us] with the knowledge of his will through all spiritual wisdom and understanding" (Col. 1:9). In a nutshell Paul is praying that the church will know God's philosophy rather than the philosophy of the times.

C. S. Lewis, in his book *Miracles,* describes two kinds of truth.[4] First, there is the Naturalist who says, "This universe is all there is. Only what I can see, touch, taste, hear or smell is real!" Then there is the Supernaturalist who believes, "There is a lot more to it than that . . . God is really there. He created this universe from the outside and entered it in the person of Jesus Christ!" Lewis didn't talk about "postmodernism" because the term didn't exist then. But the postmodernist would say, "You are both correct. Truth can be based on empirical evidence and it can be based on faith. You can all have your own truths. And I can have mine too."

Colossians stands boldly in opposition to such postmodernist statements. Paul's message to Colossae is not Christ *and*—it is Christ *only*. We cannot have Christ and anything (whether another philosophy or an additional religion). You must have Christ only. He is the one and the only one. As Eugene Peterson renders the last verse of chapter one, "Christ! No more, no less. That's what I'm working so hard at day after day, year after year, doing my best with the energy God so generously gives me."

If Christ is the answer, then what are the questions? Have they really changed that much? Even with a new philosophical environment like postmodernism, the critical and haunting questions of identity are still there. So we continue to ask the questions: Who am I? Why am I here? Where am I going? And the Bible says, "For in him we live and move and have our being" (Acts 17:28).

What is life all about? Paul reminds us when he says, "My purpose is that they may be encouraged in heart and united in love, so that they may have the full riches of complete understanding, in order that they may know the mystery of God, namely, Christ, in whom are hidden all the treasures of wisdom and knowledge" (Col. 2:2-3).

Ultimately, the goal of any philosophy is to discover "the treasures of wisdom and knowledge." Is that possible? Yes—but only through Christ. Jesus is still the answer!

Questions For Discussion

1. What are the big questions facing our society today?

2. What have been the big changes you have seen in your world as we have entered the twenty-first century?

3. Describe the major differences of the Medieval, Modern and Postmodern periods.

4. What are the "Four Posts of Postmodernism"?

5. In what ways have you seen the "Fall of the West"? How do you think this affects Christianity?

6. What are some activities that were considered illegitimate by our society but now are considered legitimate? What is your opinion of the changes?

7. Where has control been lost in your world because of the "intellectual marketplace"? Has this been good or bad in your experience?

8. What is "deconstruction"? Where have you observed examples of it?

9. Do you think Christianity can fit into a postmodern world? Explain.

10. Read Colossians 2:8-9. How is the book of Colossians relevant to our postmodern world?

11. Read Colossians 1:1-14. What attitude does Paul have for a church engulfed in a culture with a bad philosophical base?

12. What answers does Christ provide for our postmodern world?

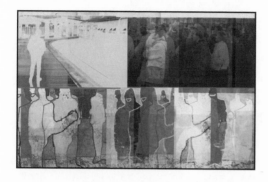

2

Celebrate Reconciliation

Can I Know Anything for Sure Anymore?

"Jesus Loves Me"—it's the first song I remember learning in church. On second thought, it's the first song I learned anywhere. Even today, when I remember my own children singing that familiar verse, "Jesus loves me this I know, for the Bible tells me so," I flash back to the old smells and sounds of my childhood church. I can still recall where my youthful first steps in faith began.

As we teach these simple songs and ideas to our children, they provide similar foundational memories of church and God that we hope will never leave them. But the question is: are these child-hood songs and foundational memories enough to hold us in good stead as we grow and mature and eventually leave home or go off to college?

My parents always expected me to go to Abilene Christian College in West Texas. But all my friends urged me to go to Texas Tech. I can still hear people at church pleading with me, "Don't go to that big, bad state university. You will lose your faith. Your Christianity will wear off." But why, I thought? Was I not given a big enough faith to withstand university life? If I got around thinking people, people with critical intelligence, would my faith not hold up?

Now that I have children of my own, I can better appreciate the apprehensions people have concerning the influences of outside forces on a youthful, untried faith. It scares me to think that my children or any children may not have what it takes to survive college, let alone the secular world, with their faith intact. Maybe we aren't teaching them enough. But, then again, maybe we need to have faith in "faith" itself. As Christians we should not be afraid of the realities of life. We must believe that our faith can hold up even in the intellectually stimulating world of academia or the hustle and bustle of the secular world.

As a matter of fact, some of the most intelligent and well-informed people I've ever met are at church. At the church where I minister, there are more graduate degrees than most any other secular organization of similar size or economic makeup. Indeed, we are as intellectually astute in our Christian communities as in most other segments of our society.

However, it is not the intellectual battle that I fear. Christians can stand their ground in any battle of wits today. What is more troublesome is the postmodern trend in today's society which does not allow Christians to defend their faith anymore.

As author Jim Leffel has noted, "We live in strange times. When I was in college twenty years ago, Christianity was under fire because it was thought to be unscientific—and consequently, untrue. Today, Christianity is widely rejected, not because it [has been] critically examined and found wanting, but merely because it claims to be true."[1] Being a Christian in this postmodern world may be more challenging than at any time since the first-century beginnings of our faith.

Notice the following photographs. If I asked you to tell me which one was "postmodern," whom would you pick: Eddie Vedder (of the alternative/rock group "Pearl Jam") or Abigail Van Buren (of "Dear Abby" fame)?

Eddie Vedder
of Pearl Jam

Abigail Van Buren

The answer is not as obvious as it seems. The correct answer is that both Mr. Vedder and Dear Abby should be considered "postmodern." Of course, most of us would pick a grunge rock musician over a newspaper columnist to reflect the signs of our times. What could be more postmodern than Pearl Jam's "No Way" where Vedder sings, "I'll quit trying to make a difference. No way."

But on the other hand look at Dear Abby. At first blush she may seem to be an old fogey, representing a certain older-generational view of society. But one of her recent columns prompted a telling response from a reader.[2] "Your answer to the woman who complained that her relatives were always arguing with her about religion was ridiculous. You advised her to simply declare the subject off-limits. Are you suggesting that people talk about only trivial, meaningless subjects so as to avoid a potential controversy? . . . It is arrogant to tell people there are subjects they may not mention in your presence. You could have suggested she learn enough about her relatives' cult to show them the errors contained in its teaching."[3]

Although it is commendable of Dear Abby to print her readers' challenging responses to her columns, it is perhaps more telling to note Abby's response to her responder: "In my view, the height of arrogance is to attempt to show people the 'errors' in the religion of their choice."

There is perhaps nothing more postmodern than this statement from Abigail Van Buren. Eddie Vedder himself couldn't have sung it any better.

An Old Song for Postmodern Times

As we have seen, many of the answers to postmodern problems can be found in the book of Colossians, as it too was dealing with a wrong philosophy that had infiltrated the church. In Colossians 2:8 the Apostle Paul warns, "See to it that no one takes you captive through hollow and deceptive philosophy, which depends on human tradition and the basic principles of this world rather than on Christ."

No sooner had Jesus risen from the grave than people were saying he was not divine. Some said he wasn't dead. Others proposed that the body was stolen. Some began to say that it really wasn't God on the cross. These challenges to Jesus' identity hit directly at the essence of Christianity.

In one of today's Broadway musicals, an important dilemma might be answered in a song. At church we might turn to a hymn to give us a clearer insight into a theological theme. Paul appears to be doing the same thing in Colossians 1:15-23. Scholars tend to think these verses were written as a song. And indeed they are quite lyrical. However, scholars are not in agreement as to whether Paul wrote the verses himself or whether he used a familiar lyric to make a point.

15 He is the image of the invisible God, the firstborn over all creation.

16 For by him all things were created: things in heaven and on earth, visible and invisible, whether thrones or powers or rulers or authorities; all things were created by him and for him.

17 He is before all things, and in him all things hold together.

18 And he is the head of the body, the church; he is the beginning and the firstborn from among the dead, so that in everything he might have the supremacy.

19 For God was pleased to have all his fullness dwell in him,

20 and through him to reconcile to himself all things, whether things on earth or things in heaven, by making peace through his blood, shed on the cross.

Then, continuing the musical analogy, Paul makes his point based on the song's meaning.

21 Once you were alienated from God and were enemies in your minds because of your evil behavior.

22 But now he has reconciled you by Christ's physical body through death to present you holy in his sight, without blemish and free from accusation—

23 if you continue in your faith, established and firm, not moved from the hope held out in the gospel. This is the gospel that you heard and that has been proclaimed to every creature under heaven, and of which I, Paul, have become a servant. (Colossians 1:15-23)

If you analyze the meaning of the song, here is what it's saying:

Jesus is just like God (v.15)
He created everything (v. 16)
He is timeless (v.17)
He holds everything together (v. 17)
He is the head of the church (v. 18)

And then perhaps the most radical statement of all:

All of God was in this one man (v.19)

What is Paul saying? He is making the bold statement that Jesus is God!

People today are not arguing that God doesn't exist. It seems that the "God is dead" movement has pretty much died its own death. On campus today Jesus' existence is not being attacked—he is just one of the options. As a result the issue has become, "Is Jesus one of the options or is Jesus the one and only?"

Of these two views of Jesus, the Apostle Paul takes the second view. Jesus is not just one of many; he is the one.

Paul's conviction harmonizes with what Jesus actually claimed about himself. Jesus said, "I and the Father are one" (John 10:30). And further in the same text, Jesus answered: "Don't you know me, Philip, even after I have been among you such a long time? Anyone who has seen me has seen the Father. How can you say, 'Show us the Father'?" (John 14:9).

But perhaps the most controversial and problematic passage in the Bible for postmodernists is John 14:6, where Jesus states, "I am the way and the truth and the life. No one comes to the Father except through me" (John 14:6). The real problem for postmodernists is Jesus' use of the term "the way." If he had used the phrase "I am 'a' way," all would have been fine. The problem is his use of the word "the," as in "the only way." This means that Jesus is the one and only, exclusive way to the Father. How bold and presumptuous can a statement be? Can a claim so exclusive be true?

Postmodernism says, "One God is as good as another." Jesus says, "I am the way." Other world religions say, "All roads lead to the same place." But Jesus says "There is one road."

The Colossian song cited by Paul says that "in everything He is to have the supremacy." Therefore, Paul is saying that all religions and religious leaders are not equal. Postmodernists, of course, have a big problem with Paul's way of thinking. But, believe it or not, this is also a huge problem in the church. As George Barna states, "Larger proportions of born-again Christians and people who attend evangelical churches concur with [the] sentiment that all religions are equally valid paths to the same god, than [those who] reject it." Is it any wonder that most churches aren't evangelistic? Many don't even believe that people are lost.

The Errors Of Her Way

Let's go back to Dear Abby. Her statement was, "In my view, the height of arrogance is to attempt to show people the 'errors' in the religion of their choice." Let's examine this statement for the two huge errors it contains.

First, it is saying that entering into religious controversy is arrogant. The statement is saying that we should not be truth seekers. It says we are arrogant to think we can find the truth. And if we believe that we have found it, we are arrogant to think that we should be evangelistic and share those beliefs. To the postmodernist this is like stating you are better than another.

In the movie "At Play in the Fields of the Lords," a conversation takes place between an Amazon Indian and a Christian missionary. The Indian says, "If the Lord made Indians the way they are, who are you people to make them different?" The postmodernist would say, "What gives you the right to make anyone different?"

The second error in Abby's above-noted statement is that "personal choice is the basis for truth." This statement rejects not only objective evidence but also subjective spiritual experience as a sufficient basis for truth. Rather, this way of thinking ultimately bases truth simply on personal choice. In other words, there is no such thing as the truth. Thus the difficulty is evident when Jesus says, "I am the truth."

In postmodernism we are to leave everyone alone and celebrate diversity, not try to change it. You can see the bumpersticker everywhere, "Celebrate Diversity." Diversity sounds good if it means not being prejudiced. But in postmodern culture, that is not what it means. It means buying into a philosophy that says one truth is as good as another. Paul, in contrast, is calling for reconciliation to the real truth: "and through him to reconcile to himself all things, whether things on earth or things in heaven, by making peace through his blood, shed on the cross" (Col. 1:20).

The heart of the Christian message is not the celebration of diversity. Rather, it calls for very different people to be reconciled as one in Jesus. We are not to be the generation of diversity but the generation of reconciliation.

There is a famous story of Karl Barth, the great writer of Christian theology, who, as he lay on his death bed, was asked what was the greatest truth he had learned during his lifetime. His only response was, "Jesus loves me this I know, for the Bible tells me so." That simple line from a child's song, the first song many of us ever sang, says a lot. It says: there is a God, and the God of the universe has entered this world. And most importantly it says: He loves you. How can you know? Because the Bible tells you so.

Questions For Discussion

1. What are some places where Christians have been dismissed as not having enough intellectual prowess in the modern age?

2. Where is Christianity today being dismissed because of its exclusive claims to truth?

3. Why are Christians seen as arrogant in our current society? Give an example of how this has happened to you.

4. Read Colossians 1:15-23. What is the unique genre of this scripture? What does the passage say about the uniqueness of Jesus?

5. Read John 14:6. How does this verse separate Christianity from other world religions?

6. What are the ramifications for a society when personal choice becomes the basis for truth?

7. What does "Celebrate Diversity" mean? Why is it a popular message today? How can it become problematic for Christianity?

8. Is the Bible still a valid source of knowledge in a postmodern world? Explain how it is and why it will be difficult to get people to accept it.

3

The Truth Is
More Than Out There

What's too scary on television? As a parent I always worry about what our kids are watching on television. At times I even worry about what is too scary for me. One night my wife, Barbie, and I were diligently trying to decide if The X Files was too scary for our kids (it was definitely too scary for me that night). When we asked our son Jeremy, his answer was surprising. He said, "It's not the show that scares me. It's the theme song."

Remembering my son's comment, I once told my congregation that I wanted to spice things up and have a scary sermon. I was going to open up the service with that infamous theme from the X Files. With one of those legal-type disclaimers, the faint of heart were told they could wait in the foyer until the music was over. Then it started. The eerie music and video clips from the opening sequence were shown on the big screen in our auditorium. At the end of the video the congregation knew why I did it. Frozen on the screen was the message: "The Truth is Out There."

I love this statement. It is a theme of this book. When I see this statement on television week after week, I just want to jump up from my couch and yell, "Yes!"

If you stop to think about it, Christians in a postmodern world can identify with the X-Files agent, Fox Mulder. It seems as if he is the only one on the show who is not postmodern. Mulder works for the FBI and is on a quest to find his sister who has disappeared. He thinks there is something supernatural about her childhood disappearance. There has to be an explanation; the truth is out there. Mulder will not stop until he finds out what really happened. He risks his and partner Agent Scully's life every week because he is seeking the truth.

Most everybody else in Mulder's postmodern world operates on the belief system that there is no truth out there. In episode after episode Mulder runs into people who try to keep him from finding the truth. Still, he pursues it.

Even though X-Files deals mainly with the weird and paranormal, I can relate to Agent Mulder. My world is also full of truth-denying people. Although Christians are saying that the real truth is out there, the rest of the world is not buying into our belief system that says there is an explanation for everything around us. And even I, like Mulder, have to ask, "Will it make any sense when I find it?"

In my world people often try to stop or discourage my search for the truth. Others attempt with the best of their ability to hide the truth from me. But most people just think I'm a little too fanatical, like Agent Mulder.

The X-Files truly catches up the postmodern blending of science with mysticism. But in spite of that, I like the fact that someone is actually pursuing truth, even if he is not going the right direction. It's better than someone who has given up on finding the truth altogether.

When it comes to the source and nature of truth today, there are many worldviews. Let's look at four of these. The basic postmodern worldview asserts that . . .

"The Truth Is Not Out There."

In other words, the postmodernist takes the view that everything is relative. There is no one true story. We all have our viewpoints, but no one has the truth.

The worldview which is closer to the Christian position, but still not quite the same is . . .

"The Truth Is Out There (Somewhere)."

This kind of statement usually comes from the seeker who believes indeed that truth is out there somewhere, but he or she hasn't found it yet. This is the view that says every once in a while we humans are visited by the truth. Periodically, a strange event happens. The revelation makes us think that perhaps something truthful is out there. It is just enough to keep us looking.

Right when we are about to give up, a clue appears. A hint is revealed that seems to point us to the truth (like one of Fox Mulder's childhood flashbacks or the man with the cigarette)—but never enough to quite solve the mystery.

Another interesting—and common—worldview says that . . .

"The Truth Is In Here."

This view holds that since we can't prove or explain the mysteries which are out there, we must assume that the answer is not out there, but rather inside each of us. Many today, including some Christians, have been turning to various Eastern religions and mysticism. The key difference between Western and Eastern religions lies in this view as to where the truth is. Christians say the truth is out there. Eastern religions say the truth is in here (inside). As a result, they must take a look inward to find the truth. Whether by contemplation, meditation or saying "Ahmmm," they look inward rather than outward to discover the truth.

Many in the West would consider themselves far from Buddhism, yet their view of truth is not dissimilar. Sidhartha Gautama was born in 560 BC in Nepal. At age 29 he became dissatisfied with his luxury and religion. Gautama swore he would not move until he found what he was searching for. After sitting under a tree for 40 days and nights, he said that he experienced Nirvana. He claimed to have found salvation. Gautama came to be known as "Buddha" or "The Enlightened One," and began teaching that others could find this state of Nirvana by following what he called "The Four Noble Truths."

Although some of these truths are similar to the ones Jesus espoused in the Sermon on the Mount, Buddha's truths were achieved by self-discovery. He taught that a person could discover the truths internally and achieve them by one's own power.

The lesson to be learned from these different worldviews is that any system or law which has a skewed perspective of the truth will ultimately not produce enlightenment or success but disillusionment and failure. In the postmodern world where many have turned to mysticism and New Age religion, the message of the gospel stands out as being different. The Christian message is not saying that the truth is in here. Or at least not initially.

The Christian worldview asserts that truth is inside us but not as the starting place of discovery. The Christian worldview says that . . .

"The Truth Out There Is In Here."
Let us take a closer look at Colossians to discover where the Christian truth is actually located.

24 Now I rejoice in what was suffered for you, and I fill up in my flesh what is still lacking in regard to Christ's afflictions, for the sake of his body, which is the church.

25 I have become its servant by the commission God gave me to present to you the word of God in its fullness—

26 the mystery that has been kept hidden for ages and generations, but is now disclosed to the saints.

27 To them God has chosen to make known among the Gentiles the glorious riches of this mystery, which is Christ in you, the hope of glory. (Colossians 1:24-27)

The Apostle Paul in this passage does say that there is a mystery and that it has been hidden for ages and generations. The truth is indeed out there, just like Mulder's theme for life, but it is difficult to perceive. But Paul also says that it is not hidden out there anymore. It has been disclosed to the saints. It has been revealed.

What is the truth that Paul is talking about? What is the mystery? What is it out there that explains it all? It is Christ Himself. Through Jesus and by the revelation of the Word of God everything has been made known. But surprisingly, there is more!

Paul also notes that, "To them God has chosen to make known among the Gentiles the glorious riches of this mystery, which is Christ in you, the hope of glory" (Col. 1:27). Therefore, the truth is out there and it has been disclosed. But he adds that the truth is "in you." The mystery of God is now in all Christians. The key is this: you do not get to the truth by starting on the inside. You must start "out there" first. Initially, we must seek beyond ourselves.

Not only is the mystery out there, this truth is out there for all to discover. As Paul notes, the mystery has been revealed. It is as if someone has read the last page of this mystery to us. We know the answer to "who done it?"

So the question is, "Should we still seek the truth like Agent Mulder?" Of course. We never stop seeking God's truth. But as Christian seekers, we are certain that the truth is out there. We can find it because the mystery has been revealed through God's only Son, Jesus Christ.

Jesus confirmed our truth-seeking when he said, "Ask and it will be given to you; seek and you will find; knock and the door will be opened to you" (Matt. 7:7). Isaiah the prophet similarly taught, "Seek the LORD while he may be found; call on him while he is near" (Isa. 55:6). There is a place where you can find Jesus. And there are places where he will be harder to find. But you can seek him right where you are. Jeremiah gives us the clue: "You will seek me and find me when you seek me with all your heart" (Jer. 29:13).

Bridging The Gap

When John wrote his gospel, there were also the Mulders of his society. They had been influenced by Greek thought. You probably remember studying the Greek gods back when you were in high school. They had names like Zeus and Hermes. But none of us ever believed in these gods. As John was writing, the people had also lost faith in these gods. But still, they thought the truth was out there. Something was out there if only they could find it. Then and only then would everything make sense. The Greeks had a name for what was out there. Their name for this truth was the "logos."

So John starts his gospel with an analogy that would have been totally in agreement with the philosophical thinking of his day—that there is truth out there. He begins:

1 In the beginning was the Word (the logos), and the Word was with God, and the Word was God.

2 He was with God in the beginning.

3 Through him all things were made; without him nothing was made that has been made.

4 In him was life, and that life was the light of men. (John 1:1-4).

Notice how the teaching has a similar ring to the Colossian song of the last chapter. Then John continues: "The Word became flesh and made his dwelling among us. We have seen his glory, the glory of the One and Only, who came from the Father, full of grace and truth" (John 1:14). He then concludes his thought about this rationale behind the universe called the *logos* with: "No one has ever seen God, but God the One and Only, who is at the Father's side, has made him known" (John 1:18).

John defines Jesus as the *logos* who was with God and then becomes man. He is the truth who was out there but now he has revealed himself and been known in the form of a man.

The Greek philosopher Heraclitus gave one of the earliest definitions of the word "logos." He said that logos was that which holds contradictions and opposites together. His definition is analogous to the contradictions and opposites which exist in our own postmodern world.[1]

For example, churches are becoming smaller and larger. We have not only seen the resurrection of numerous house-churches but also many so-called megachurches. Televisions are getting both smaller and larger at the same time. The world is throwing away more than ever and at the same time recycling more than ever. People are becoming more overweight and more anorexic than ever before. The less you get paid, the harder you have to work. The more global we become, the more locally we have to think. Businesses are merging into giant, consolidated companies, and small, independent companies are making millions on the Internet. New houses are bigger, while family sizes are getting smaller. The best selling cosmetic products these days are both natural hair products and hair coloring kits. More and more people long to belong and yet they hate to be lumped and claimed. While scientific achievement is at an all time high, more and more people are looking for miracles.

We are all living in a world of contradictions, and yet something is holding it all together. Heraclitus claims that this societal glue is the *logos*.

But in reality, as John notes in his Gospel, it is Christ who is the *logos* or glue holding together our world of contradictions and opposites. The mystery is not just that he brings us to himself, but that he brought both Jews and Gentiles together; not just one group, culture or race, but all citizens of the earth. Who would have thought anyone could bring us all together?

Heraclitus used the illustration of a stick to explain his definition of the *logos*. He would pick up a stick. When he demonstrated that the ends were unconnected, he would conclude that the stick was worthless. Then he would display a stick with both ends connected in the form of a harp or a bow, revealing its value as a tool or a teaching aid. By bridging both useless ends of the stick the entire implement became valuable. A bridged stick could be used either as a weapon to kill a savage beast or a musical harp to soothe a savage beast.

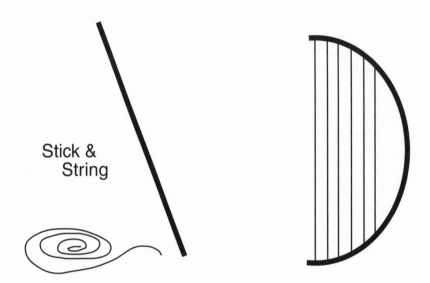

Stick & String

It is in this Christ-centered idea of connecting things to create *logos* that the Christian finds great hope during our postmodern age. Even with all the diversity of a postmodern world, when opposites are combined under the power of Christ as the *logos*, the newly created whole can produce harmony.

The main problem with our postmodern world is that many are trying to bridge the opposites and contradictions in our culture without the everlasting truth that is in Jesus Christ. As the world attempts to create this postmodern bridge, it continues to create weapons of destruction rather than instruments of harmony. The despair and destruction we witness all around us in the postmodern age are confirming this tragic reality.

In the face of this situation, Christians are called to build bridges with the *logos*—Jesus—in order to hear the beautiful music that a heavenly instrument of harmony can create.

What then will the future hold for the postmodern world? Will there be more destruction or will there be healing? Will it be destructive bows or heavenly harps?

These are the best of times for any Christian ministry and, at the same time, the worst of times. In this postmodern world of opposites and contradictions, Jesus is the only one who can bridge the gap. He is the only one who can bring the truth out there into a personal relationship.

The truth is indeed out there. But the truth is also in here. The real truth of Christ is both out there and in here in the heart.

Questions For Discussion

1. In what areas do people still go against the culture in their search for truth?

2. Give some examples of people who believe "the truth is not out there."

3. Where are some of the places people look to find tidbits of truth?

4. What are some postmodern examples of searching for truth by looking inside oneself?

5. Read Colossians 1:24-27. What is the mystery of God according to Paul in this passage?

6. Read John 1:1-14. What was the meaning of the *logos* in the first century? How was Jesus the *logos*?

7. What are the contradicting and opposite areas that need to be connected in our current culture? How can Jesus do this?

I'm Fine

How are you doing? Fine.

Isn't that what you always hear? When you ask someone how they are doing, the answer usually is "Fine."

Fine is like the ultimate in being. It is what we say to be accepted by another person. Maybe it is a cop-out. Maybe it's another way to say, "Leave me alone." But it is ultimately the way our culture defines well-being: "I'm fine."

We are living in a world where everyone wants to be fine. However, if I engage you for very long with my worldview, you may not feel fine.

In the hit song, "Closer To Fine," Emily Saliers of Indigo Girls seems to be on a journey to find the truth.[1] In her search, she looks for an "insight between black and white." As she travels through philosophy and religion, Saliers only finds confusion and unappealing answers. It is as if she can't live without an answer and can't live with the one she finds. She sings, "Darkness has a hunger that's insatiable and lightness has a call that's hard to hear."

In typical postmodern fashion, she concludes with multiple truth: "There's more than one answer to these questions pointing me in a crooked line." As a result, she stops her journey for any kind of absolute and merely accepts the options that come with tolerance. What's the resolution for Indigo Girls? "The less I seek my source for some definitive—the closer I am to fine."

Few statements describe the postmodern situation better than this chorus. If "fine" is the goal, then the farther away a person gets from any absolute or definitive truth, the closer a person will be to the goal. Since everybody wants to be fine, we avoid talking about anything important or definitive that could be divisive or challenging or might require a change of thought.

Who Knows?

Can you see the difficulty for a Christian when confronting this mindset? In Christianity we are on a quest for truth. We are trying to get closer and closer to the knowledge of the truth. Now we live in a culture where people are trying to get farther and farther away from a

One of the Indigo Girls

source for knowing a definitive. In other words Christians and post-moderns are going opposite directions.

In today's postmodern world, on the one hand, spirituality is "in." But on the other hand, knowledge is "out." Why? People who pursue knowledge may end up with a definitive. As a result the big question we face as Christians today does not revolve around, "Is faith valid?" Now the big question is, "How can you know?"

Let me illustrate this shift with a recent conversation I had while flying from Dallas to Seattle.[2] A young Korean businessman sat down beside me. After a little talk I learned that he was from Seoul, had an international business in China, played golf, and was going to move near Fort Worth, Texas.

Now it was his turn. He glanced at the book on postmodernism that I was reading and asked the standard questions: "Where have you been?" and "What do you do?" I told him that I was a minister and a professor. Then I explained that I had just been in Amarillo working with the Christian Relief Fund which helped needy children around the world.

In the next instant the man had his hand extended and slapped himself for being so bad. He told me that he had grown up in Seoul where there were many churches, and yet had never gone to one. His wife had asked him to go many times, but he never did. My new friend resolved to do some quick confession and penance.

After slapping himself for not going to church, my new friend offered me money to help the orphans and said that when he moved to Texas he would go to church where my good friend Rick Atchley preaches. And just to seal the deal we decided to get together and play golf.

Having all the important things behind us, he decided to take a nap. I said that I needed to get back to my book on postmodernism and to think a little bit.

As he nodded off and I was reading, the man in the seat behind us started talking to a college student. This man had the loudest voice I have ever heard and was really obnoxious, both in tone and vocabulary. My friend from Korea woke up. I couldn't concentrate. And we just rolled our eyes at each other. We both knew what each other was thinking.

In a few minutes we discerned the mission of the man behind us. He was trying to recruit this student into some multi-level marketing company. And he talked loud enough so if there was anyone else on the plane interested they would hear about it too. I was not eavesdropping—there was was simply no way to avoid the conversation.

The man told the student that he could make a fortune in a very short time. In fact, it would take only a few hours a week. He probably was going to get so rich that he wouldn't even need to finish his business degree. My new friend from Korea looked at me and shook his head. He knew the price of success in business.

Well, I wondered why this college student was listening to this two-hour sales pitch so politely. Then I got it. When the man finally paused, this young student tried to give his testimony. He was a Christian. He was thinking, "If I listen to this man, he will listen to me."

Hardly anything had come out of his mouth before the student was interrupted. The man proclaimed that he already went to a New Age church. Next, he said that he followed Buddha, Mohammed and Jesus. They were all good moral teachers. In fact, he said, "That Jesus was 'right on' in what he said. He just wasn't the only one." Then he added, "We just don't buy into that death for our sins and the coming back from the dead stuff!"

That's when I turned and shook my head to my Korean friend. I knew the price of salvation in religion.

The student didn't know what to say. He wasn't prepared for this response. He must have looked devastated because everything became silent. And after the first bit of quiet in about three hours, the man said as a way of concession, "But maybe he did do that death and life thing. Who knows?"

That's when a voice came up from the seat in front of him. You know who it was.

"I do!"

Who knows? That was the question of the flight and of our generation. Two opinions. Two directions. Are they of equal value? Who knows?

Who knows? I do.

How do I know? I told you earlier. I learned it in the first Sunday School class I ever attended. How do I know? How do I have a basis for knowledge in a postmodern world? How do I know that my story is true?

"Jesus loves me this I know, for the Bible tells me so."

The Bible gives me a basis for knowing the validity of my faith in the story of Jesus. That little song not only gives me the answer for the biggest question of my life but also tells me where I can go for knowledge.

Fancy Talk

The problem in postmodernism lies not so much in religion as in knowing a definitive. People are fine with us being religious. It is when we say "we know" that problems occur. Postmoderns have no basis for knowledge in our world today.

David Tao sings, "Where will you be when you get where you're going? How will you know that you've taken the right way? Nothing on earth can satisfy your deepest needs. Who can be sure of anything today?"[3]

In a postmodern world, no one can be sure of anything. But it goes deeper than that. No one can tolerate anyone who is sure of something. When tolerance has become the chief virtue of a society, the only thing we can't tolerate is intolerance. As a result, a belief in a definitive only looks like intolerance of other options.

What was the man behind me on the airplane really giving the young college student? Fancy talk. Let Paul explain:

1 I want you to know how much I am struggling for you and for those at Laodicea, and for all who have not met me personally.

2 My purpose is that they may be encouraged in heart and united in love, so that they may have the full riches of complete understanding, in order that they may know the mystery of God, namely, Christ,

3 in whom are hidden all the treasures of wisdom and knowledge.

4 I tell you this so that no one may deceive you by fine-sounding arguments. (Colossians 2:1-4)

I really like the way verse four is translated in the *Contemporary English Version*: "I tell you these things to keep you from being fooled by fancy talk." What is "fancy talk"? In the first century this was a philosophical word that meant "talk without certainty." That was the problem with the man on the plane, and it is the problem with the philosophy of our age.

Why did my Korean friend shake his head when he heard the loud man telling the young man about the business opportunity? He knew that there was no certainty that he was going to get rich. My friend knew economics and business. Later, I shook my head because I knew that there was no certainty to his religion.

"Who knows?" he said.

Paul believed that he knew. In another letter from prison, Paul unequivocally stated his assurance of knowledge: "That is why I am suffering as I am. Yet I am not ashamed, because I know whom I have believed, and am convinced that he is able to guard what I have entrusted to him for that day" (2 Tim. 1:12).

The mystery of Paul's message to the Colossians involves incarnation. God visits us—not in some subjective or simply spiritual way but in a physical, tangible way. The Truth out there is now in here. That is the message, and the choice is this—the incarnation or fancy talk.

Which do you choose? A message based on substance and

history or one based on no certainty—one that you just happen to like better?

The message of Colossians is that Christianity is not just another philosophy without certainty. It is a religion based on revelation. God Himself is manifested in flesh. The message is revealed in the Word. And the message is indwelled by the Spirit.

Francis Schaeffer, the American theologian who lived in Switzerland, used a mountain climbing analogy to illustrate the character of Christian truth.[4] A climber in the Alps upon reaching a pinnacle of the mountain found himself in a snowstorm. He knew that he soon had either to descend the mountain or freeze to death. He also knew that there was a safe way down and another way over a cliff that would lead to certain death. But he didn't know the way.

What could the climber do? He could just run and take a blind leap of faith. He would be off the pinnacle and below the storm. But he might also be dead.

Suppose, however, that he heard a voice. The voice came from someone below him. It told him which way to jump. If he jumped toward the voice, he was told, it would be only a small leap and safety would await him.

Would he leap? Maybe. But wouldn't he first ask, "Who are you?" Was the person directing him experienced? Had he been there before? Did he really know where he was? Was this a friend or an enemy telling him what to do?

If he jumped, certainly it would be a leap of faith. However, it would not be a blind leap of faith. No, it would be a guided leap of faith.

As Christians we are asked by God to make a leap of faith. But this leap is anything but blind. It is a guided leap of faith. We have the word of God to guide us. And we have Jesus who has been here before and truly knows where we are. Most importantly, our advice is coming from a friend who loves us. As Francis Schaeffer said, "He is there. And He is not silent."

It still takes faith. But it's a guided leap. Faith is not some kind of blind leap without any certainty.

Let's go back to the conversation on the airplane. What really happened there? I put in a good word for Jesus that day. Did the man behind me accept it? That I don't know. I doubt it. But I do know that God was pleased, that the man had an opportunity to hear, and three out of four of us walked away knowing Jesus died for us and rose from the dead. And that ain't half bad.

Questions For Discussion

1. Why do you think people today usually answer "fine" when they are asked, "How are you doing?"

2. Why is "fine" seen as getting away from a definitive in postmodernism?

3. Have you ever talked to someone who simply thought Jesus was a good, moral teacher but no more than that? Tell about it. Why is this not acceptable for Christians?

4. Explain how religion is acceptable today but not absolute knowledge of a truth.

5. Read Colossians 2:1-4. Where does Paul say that we get our source of knowledge?

6. What is fancy talk? Where have you heard fancy talk in your community?

7. How can we speak with certainty about Jesus in a world that denies certainty?

8. What is the difference in blind faith and guided faith? Give examples of each.

The Carousel of Regress

The first time I went to Disneyworld was in 1975. When most people go to Disneyworld, they spend all day riding as many rides as they can in order to get their money's worth. Then, right before closing time, everyone goes back to ride their favorite ride several more times. When Barbie and I were there, people were waiting in long lines outside the Pirates of the Caribbean, Space Mountain, and the Haunted House trying to get in as many last minute rides as possible. Not so with the Jones family. We had a short line because Barbie's favorite attraction at Disneyworld back then was an exhibit called "The G.E. Carousel of Progress."

Why did she choose the Carousel of Progress? It had a cool theme song. Barbie always opts for music over adventure. I guess if memories count for something, maybe it wasn't such a bad choice. Because after all these years that catchy little tune still rings in my ear: "Now is the time. Now is the best time. Now is the best time of your life." Do you remember it?

But things never stay the same, do they? On our family's most recent vacation trip back to Disneyworld, we looked everywhere. But the "Carousel of Progress" was no longer there. Sure we missed the ride. But maybe its absence was significant in another way.

It's not that I'm overly nostalgic. In fact, the loss was much greater for Barbie. To my amazement, she could still remember and sing every word from the theme song: "Now is the time. Now is the best time. Now is the best time of your life." In place of the carousel, a new structure had been erected. But things were different now.

I'm sure we'll get over it some day. But it got me thinking—the Carousel of Progress was now gone. If there was one thing that our traditional modern world was built upon, it had been progress. Now that we are smack-dab in the middle of the postmodern world, is progress no longer our most important business? If so, how did we get here? What happened to the old modern world? Could it be that we have witnessed the death of the modern "myth of progress"?

How Did Modernism Die?

Let's examine why the modern world fell. Certainly not everyone will agree with my point of view. But as Christians we need to see as clearly as possible what happened. I like to think of the modern world falling in 1992, the year we celebrated the 500-year anniversary of Columbus' famous voyage.

An interesting thing happened before the celebration party. No one wanted to tell the story the way it had been told in the past. Suddenly, Columbus wasn't seen as a hero anymore. And the discovery story wasn't told from Columbus' point of view any longer. Historians began to tell the story from what had previously been deemed a minority viewpoint. This change in point of view may represent the last nail in the coffin of our modern age.

If modernism started to close in 1992, then when did it actually start? Perhaps it began with what historians call the Age of Enlightenment (around the eighteenth century). But, in deference to Christopher Columbus, I like to date the start of the modern world with the year 1492. For it was in "Fourteen hundred and ninety-two when Columbus sailed the ocean blue" that we saw the birth of the progress myth. Others would say the progress myth goes all the way back to Egypt and Greece where the deepest roots of Western culture lie. But no story embodies the progress myth more than Columbus' discovery of the Americas.

Columbus started with a gigantic dream. His goal centered around a new ocean-trading route to Asia. He did not look backwards to what was known; rather he looked forward in an attempt to gaze upon the unknown. But it didn't stop there. The story of progress was repeated over and over again, marking the steady advancement of modern society—until 1992. It was at this approximate time in history when people stopped telling the old story and started telling a different one.

The progress myth of Columbus closely parallels one particular biblical story. This brief narrative starts with an unprecedented and adventurous human vision—a vision that does not rely on the supernatural at all but rather on human efforts alone.

Someone has a dream. And that someone is able to promote this dream in such a way that everyone agrees they are going to go where man has never been before. This, of course, is the Old Testament story of the Tower of Babel. "Come, let us build ourselves a city, with a tower that reaches to the heavens, so that we may make a name for ourselves and not be scattered over the face of the whole earth" (Gen. 11:4).

The vision of Babel is not that far off from the modern dream of the Carousel of Progress—the building of a new world order with grand and unified societal goals in order that we could sing, "Now is the best time of your life." The builders of Babel had two progressive distinctives in their vision for modernity. First, they wanted "to boldly go where no one had gone before." They wanted to "be somebody." They were after fame and fortune. Bigger was better. The sky, and maybe even God, was the limit.

Second, they wanted "to be one." Instead of fragmentation, it was a call to "come together." Any barriers that hindered social or cultural unity were to come down as they built their tower. Instead of recognizing their differences, they had the grand vision of uniting the world into a single social order. It was a bold step toward social progress.

This Old Testament vision parallels the vision of modernism. Modernists also planned to reach for heights no one had scaled before. They wanted to see a single world order where everyone could be famous or self-actualized, on the one hand, and united with a common bond, on the other. According to J. Richard Middleton and Brian Walsh, the vision of progress grew in Western culture through three levels.[1] Imagine a modern tower of Babel constructed with three floors.

The first floor of modernism was Science. Starting with the scientific revolution of the sixteenth and seventeenth centuries and continuing through modern-day America, science lay at the heart of progress. We were continually trying to understand our world through scientific advancements. We put our hope in the knowledge that came through experiments and tests. We came to believe that

(The Tower of Babel, by Pieter Brueghel)

science would always bring one more breakthrough that would give us just the knowledge we needed to solve our problems.

The second story of the modern Tower of Babel was Technology. As the eighteenth century ushered in the Age of Enlightenment, society began to reap the fruits of the Scientific Revolution of the previous century. Thus the Industrial Revolution was born. Machines were made to create a better and easier world. Scientific understanding began being applied for social benefit. We now could not only understand our world but also control it. As a result, technology fit perfectly as the second floor right above the first floor of science in this modern Tower of Babel. The first floor gave us insight. The second gave us power.

But there was an additional floor to the modern monolith. It was revealed in answer to the questions, "What did modern society use the first two floors for?" and "What did these initial stories of the tower produce?" The answer is wealth. A modern market economy began to replace the traditional feudal systems. By the start of the nineteenth century, everyone in the West wanted to

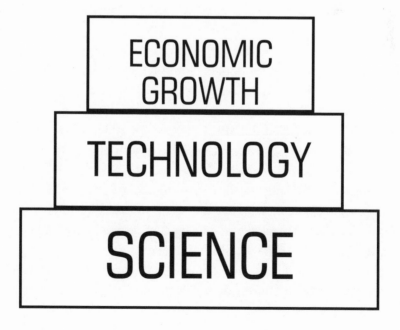

ECONOMIC GROWTH

TECHNOLOGY

SCIENCE

make a profit. As a result, Economic Growth became the third floor of the modern tower.

The Foundation Of Modernism

The carousel of progress produced a modern culture built upon science, technology and economic growth. But if we take this Tower of Babel analogy back to its foundation, down below the first floor, the question arises, "What is in the basement?" The answer to this question is—Man. Our society had not only become self-serving but also self-supported. Knowledge, power and purpose all started and continued with self. If we needed more knowledge, we could discover it ourselves. If we needed more power, we could create another machine. If we needed more purpose, we could make a little more money.

In the end modern man was like the mythological Greek figure of Atlas. Modern man was carrying the entire world of science, technology and economic growth on his own shoulders. Looking back with a Christian point of view, we should ask whether God would call this modernistic period "progress." More likely He would call it idolatry.

During the modern age, we made idols of science, technology and economic growth. Of course, some would make a case for science by pointing out that God gave us "order" to allow us to study his creation. And others will defend economic development citing what Max Weber called the "Protestant work ethic." But most all of the religious roots of modernism were eventually forgotten.

It was science that became the source of modern revelation and knowledge. Technology became the source for power to achieve whatever society wanted. And economic growth became its basic purpose, as many believed that a rising standard of living was the ultimate goal in life and the way to happiness.

There is, of course, nothing wrong with science, technology or economics in and of themselves. But at the height of modernism, they became idols or false gods. Our society should have seen the idolatrous nature of modernism from the Bible. If we had learned it from the Scriptures, perhaps we would have repented and experienced revival. But since we learned the failure of modernism from our own experience, our culture didn't know where to turn. And the result has been "postmodernism."

We now know that neither science nor technology nor even money can save us. This kind of progress did not bring us the knowledge we had anticipated. Neither did it solve our problems. And it surely did not bring the happiness we had expected.

Just as the Tower of Babel fell, the modernist myth has also fallen. And just as confusion reigned after the Tower of Babel fell, so the confusion of postmodernism is reigning now.

"But the LORD came down to see the city and the tower that the men were building. The LORD said, 'If as one people speaking the same language they have begun to do this, then nothing they plan to do will be impossible for them. Come, let us go down and confuse their language so they will not understand each other.' So the LORD scattered them from there over all the earth, and they stopped building the city. That is why it was called Babel—because there the LORD confused the lan-guage of the whole world. From there the LORD scattered them over the face of the whole earth" (Gen. 11:5-9).

When work on the ancient building stopped, there was utter confusion at Babel. There was no order to society, only groups of subcultures that could not .communicate with one another. Instead of unity there was chaos.

The condition of Babel has simply been repeated in postmodern culture. Today there is no unity in thinking or shared goals. Every ethnic group or special interest organization is trying to write the big story through its own eyes. Truth has become subjective and is based upon how each group sees it. There is no universal truth with which to check any maverick viewpoint.

When Babel fell in Old Testament times, society experienced real confusion, and they knew their situation was bad. But in our postmodern society, much of society celebrates the diversity which has resulted from the lack of universal truth. However, some of us may think that progressive modernism was good and that we should return to pre-1992 thinking. Many of us still evaluate a church by how "progressive" it is.

The problem is that we cannot go back. We cannot go back to modernism, because the real problem with the progress myth is that it never did tell the whole story. The rest of the story was that not everyone or everything actually progressed in modern society. And as some progressed, they did so at the expense of others. Postmodernism is the result of a society that had lost its proper foundation.

The carousel of progress has, indeed, stopped. We are no longer singing, "Now is the best time of your life."

The word from the apostle Paul to a similar culture was, "So then, just as you received Christ Jesus as Lord, continue to live in him, rooted and built up in him, strengthened in the faith as you were taught, and overflowing with thankfulness. See to it that no one takes you captive through hollow and deceptive philosophy, which depends on human tradition and the basic principles of this world rather than on Christ" (Col. 2:6-8).

We must all ask ourselves the questions, "Where are our roots?" and "What is the foundation we are building upon?"

We might be surprised when we honestly look at the foundation of the towers we have built. Paul in his letter to the Colossians shows the fallacy of a tower built on modernism or any human philosophy. Our strength should not be in ourselves, our personal knowledge or our own power. Neither can we depend on the progressive modernism of science, technology and economics to bring us true knowledge, power or happiness.

Our true foundation should be in "Christ only—no more, no less."

Questions For Discussion

1. When did you start noticing that the modern world seemed to be coming to a close? What events marked the end?

2. How have you seen the modern myth of progress die in your world?

3. What are some of the factors and historical events that produced the modern world?

4. What are the similarities between the building of the Tower of Babel and the rise of modernism?

5. What composed the various floors of modernism? How have you seen this to be true historically and experientially? Explain.

6. What were the results of the fall of the Tower of Babel? . . . the fall of modernism?

7. From your observations of the world, why aren't people singing "Now is the best time of your life!" as modernism comes to an end?

8. Read Colossians 2:6-8. How can both modernism and postmodernism be hollow and deceptive philosophies?

9. If you took seriously Paul's admonition to be "rooted" and "built up" in Jesus, how would your world be built?

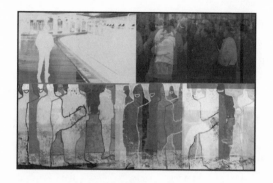

6

Tell Me the Old, Old Metanarrative

Pass It On

Attempting a simple definition of postmodernism, author Jean-Francois Lyotard stated, "Simplifying in the extreme, I define post-modernism as incredulity toward metanarratives."[1] So much for simple definitions.

It may be useful to break Lyotard's definition down into more understandable terms. "Incredulity" is the inability to believe, and a "metanarrative" is a big, all-encompassing story. Now, let's apply this definition of postmodernism to an appropriate biblical text. "So then, just as you received Christ Jesus as Lord, continue to live in him, rooted and built up in him, strengthened in the faith as you were taught, and overflowing with thankfulness" (Col. 2:6-7).

Paul points out in this passage that Jesus is our foundation. We are rooted in Him. But how do we get connected in the first place to this foundation? The traditional answer is that you receive Jesus just as it says in this scripture. But if we analyze the key concept of "receiving Jesus Christ," we may find that the common understanding is different from what Paul was teaching.

David Garland notes that "Today, evangelical Christians use this phrase (Col. 2:6-7) to mean become a Christian. Believers receive Christ by inviting him to enter their hearts and life. The verb to receive in 2:6, however, is a technical term taken over from Judaism that refers to the transmission of teaching from one person or generation to another."[2] In other words, there is a "story" that is passed on to us from others, usually from a prior generation. One might even call this story a "metanarrative." This story is like a baton which one generation is responsible for passing on to another.

Paul shares a similar baton-passing idea in 1 Corinthians: "For what I received I passed on to you as of first importance: that Christ died for our sins according to the Scriptures, that he was buried, that he was raised on the third day according to the Scriptures" (1 Cor. 15:3-4).

In our previous discussion regarding the fall of modernity, we saw that it fell not unlike the tower of Babel. Modernism was built upon science, technology, and the accumulation of wealth. And modern man was at the foundation of the structure. The proliferation of the modernist point of view was fueled by the "progress myth." This is the false premise that things would always get bigger and better in the future. It was this false notion which became the overriding "story" of modernism. The myth promoted the belief that progress would make everything better for everyone. The promise was that we could understand our world, have power over it and, of course, have lots of money. But, as we have noted, this worldview failed us. And postmodernism has been the response.

What's Wrong With Metanarratives?

Postmodernism holds to the belief that "there is no story which can give an adequate worldview to peoples."[3] The modernist story failed. Not only did the capitalistic metanarrative of the West fail but also the opposite but all-encompassing story of communism. A metanarrative is any story that attempts to supply an overall world-view. Stories that tell us how to live are metanarratives. As we have seen, it was the "progress story" embodied in Columbus' quest for the New World that taught the old world how to live. But, as post-moderns accurately point out, the development of knowledge through science, power through technology, and happiness through money does not work for the whole world, either old or new.

Postmodernists have concluded that all metanarratives fail in at least two places.[4] First, metanarratives fail the "exclusive test" in that certain groups of people inevitably get left out of the story. The post-modern theory is that no story is large enough to include all people. Second, postmodernists believe that metanarratives fail the "violence test." This is the viewpoint that the metanarrative, because it assumes universal validity, will inevitably become oppressive and vio-lent. Christopher Colombus' violence against native Americans is a good argument for metanarratives failing the violence test. These conclusions have led postmodernists to reject the possibility that any one story can be true and at the same time be truth for everyone.

As we saw in the first chapter, one of the main foundational con-clusions or posts of postmodernism is that Western society has fall-en. This, in turn, is based upon the fall of the progress myth. How did it fall? The postmodern answer is that it became too exclusive and produced violence. If the progress story is not viewed this way by the majority in America, certainly it is by most people in the world. And the real problem for Christians is that "Christianity" has become so associated with the way of the West that it too is now seen as exclusive and even to the point of producing violence. To back up this claim, many postmodernists have pointed to all the bad things that have been done "in the name of Christian faith."

Are the criticisms by postmodernists valid? Indeed, we have seen at the end of the modern era that people have been excluded and many have been the victims of violence. And in response to these observations, postmodernists have taken to the rooftops to shout their theories of what is wrong with society. What's their conclusion?

At the root of the postmodern theory of what is wrong with modernism is the entire concept of "metanarratives."

If metanarratives have caused the problem, then the loudest postmodern revisionists say that the only solution is to get rid of all metanarratives. Terry Eagleton states that, "Postmodernism signals the death of such meta-narratives whose secretly terroristic function was to ground and legitimate the illusion of a universal human history."[5] Similarly Middleton and Walsh write: "Just as all voices must be allowed to be heard in the carnival of postmodern culture, so also must we allow the proliferation of little stories in our culture. If no grand narrative is true, and if all narratives are constructed by individuals and communities, then no narrative must be privileged, and local, multiple and marginal narratives must be encouraged."[6]

The fall of metanarratives explains why our government or educational institutions can't do Christmas anymore unless it includes everything imaginable. Today, everyone has been given the right to have his or her own "small story" to the exclusion of any one "big story." Of course, this concept sounds positive at first blush. Certainly, it is good for society to hear from minorities who haven't been heard from before. We all can appreciate the lessons learned from oppressed minorities. Then again, it is quite another thing to say that no other narrative can apply to that minority, or that their minority narrative can't have an impact outside its own community. Nor would it be correct to state that everything is true within the minority narrative just because it is their narrative. This would lead to the unsolvable conundrum of why, for instance, "neo-nazism" (or any other small story) should not deserve equal attention with all other narratives.

The father of postmodernism, Frederick Nietzsche, wanted to solve this puzzle in a unique way. Since you can't have a true universal story (or metanarrative) and since society tends toward allowing only little, minority stories (none of which reflect universal truth), his solution was to get rid of all stories. Nietzsche claimed that, instead of stories, society should move toward using "aphorisms."[7] An aphorism is defined as a loosely connected and randomly sequenced comment or phrase which has no plot.

These short pithy statements are curiously similar to what our society currently calls "sound bytes." We see them every day in our information age. Just watch the television sitcoms or the nightly news. Sound bytes have become so popular in our fast-paced lives specifically because they do not have to have a plot, nor do they need to be universally true. This is what has made MTV so popular. To deal with this tension between aphorism and metanarrative, some Christians have moved closer to what might be called a "sound byte religion."

But the real problem with this line of thinking is not the "story." If metanarratives caused our cultural problems, then removing meta-narratives should solve the problems with exclusion and violence. But recent history has shown that removal of metanarratives does not solve these problems. In fact, the removal of metanarratives has even heightened exclusion and oppression in certain instances.

The fall of Communism in the Soviet Union is a stark example. For when Communism was removed from Russia giving a kick-start to postmodernism, it eliminated neither oppression nor violence. The Balkan states became a bleak reminder of this truth. Do these grim facts show that Communism and the old Soviet Union were correct? Not really, because there will be oppression and violence with or without a metanarrative. Even in South Africa, after the fall of apartheid, the oppression and violence did not end; it just transferred to bloody tribal conflicts. These continued conflicts did nothing to justify apartheid. They just show that a metanarrative is not the ultimate issue.

As a matter of fact, postmodernism is a narrative in and of itself. It has a story. Even by it own definition, "postmodernism" is a story that could not have happened without the prior plot of modernism. Postmodernism isn't just one option or little story. It isn't just one dish on the buffet table. It is the whole, all-you-can-eat table.[8]

Putting postmodernism into perspective, Walter Anderson states, "Lacking absolutes, we will have to encounter one another as people with different information, different stories, different visions—and trust the outcome."9 But can we stake our eternity on trusting the outcome? Like it or not, the truth is that people need a metanarrative. Society needs something that makes sense out of all of this. The problem is not the metanarrative. The real problem is the "sin" in all of our stories.

Another Solution: The Biblical Metanarrative

The solution to this postmodern problem does not lie in understanding postmodernism better. The answer lies in understanding God's Word better. A large part of why we got into this mixup in the first place is because of misrepresentations of the actual biblical message. Now, more than ever, we need to know what the Bible says. Especially in light of our postmodern society, we need to really understand the story of the Old Testament. The Bible is unabashedly a metanarrative. And it is being widely disregarded like other metanarratives. Why? For many reasons. But one important one is the allegation that it leads to oppression and violence.

Two monumental metanarratives run throughout the Old Testament. The first is the story of creation. In this overriding story, the Bible teaches us our roots and nature. But the second metanarrative is equally important because it tells the story of our deliverance. In the exodus God's people not only find identity but also hope.

The exodus reveals the universal metanarrative. It is the story of God coming to an oppressed people—and He loves them and rescues them. It is the defining story of the people of Israel. The Old Testament tells the story of a people who often forgot their story. And whenever God's people forget their story, they lose the truth and forget who they are. But even more importantly, they forget what to do and how to live.

To ensure their health and security, God told them to entrust to future generations a story: "*In the future, when your son asks you, 'What is the meaning of the stipulations, decrees and laws the*

LORD our God has commanded you?' tell him: 'We were slaves of Pharaoh in Egypt, but the LORD brought us out of Egypt with a mighty hand. Before our eyes the LORD sent miraculous signs and wonders— great and terrible—upon Egypt and Pharaoh and his whole household. But he brought us out from there to bring us in and give us the land that he promised on oath to our fore-fathers. The LORD commanded us to obey all these decrees and to fear the LORD our God, so that we might always prosper and be kept alive, as is the case today. And if we are careful to obey all this law before the LORD our God, as he has commanded us, that will be our righteousness'" (Deut. 6:21-25).

The metanarrative of the Bible is anything but what postmod-ernists critique as oppressive metanarratives. The real metanarrative of the Old Testament is that God is on the side of the oppressed and not the powerful. The same is also true of the Christian metanarra-tive that builds on it. Jesus is the one who heals the leper, the one who sides, not with the established leaders, whether religious or Roman, but with the helpless. Even his identity is disclosed in his lack of oppression: "So he replied to the messengers, 'Go back and report to John what you have seen and heard: The blind receive sight, the lame walk, those who have leprosy are cured, the deaf hear, the dead are raised, and the good news is preached to the poor'" (Luke 7:22).

Opponents of Christianity say that the Christian metanarrative is oppressive. But have they actually heard the true story? It is true that evil and oppressive things have been done in the name of Christianity. But is this the actual story of the Bible or a distortion? The true Christian message is not one of oppression but liberation. The biblical metanarrative is a story of peace, not of violence. The Messiah accomplished his revolution without military might. Even when he could have used his awesome power, and even when his fol-lowers begged him to do so, he refused.

But what about the criticism of exclusivity? The real problem of the Old Testament metanarrative is that it did indeed leave some people out of the story. The nation of Israel was to be a light to the nations. But seldom did their influence extend far beyond themselves. Even the first-century church struggled initially with the universality of the gospel. It was a mystery that had to be disclosed. As Paul noted in Colossians, "I have become its servant by the commission God gave me to present to you the word of God in its fullness—the mystery that has been kept hidden for ages and generations, but is now disclosed to the saints. To them God has chosen to make known among the Gentiles the glorious riches of this mystery, which is Christ in you, the hope of glory" (Col. 1:25-27).

The Bible actually gives a metanarrative that is not guilty of the two great criticisms of violence and exclusiveness. The biblical metanarrative tells a story of liberation, and not for any one group of people but for all. The philosophical answer cannot be to remove metanarratives from society. That will not solve the problem. The solution is to find a metanarrative that actually is all-encompassing for the good of all people.

Perhaps Christians have been guilty either of not knowing our own story or misrepresenting it. In African-American culture there have been two recent movements. In the spirit of postmodernism, one group has rejected metanarratives. This group has decided that the Bible is a "white book" which chronicles the progress myth and is used to oppress blacks. In this extreme, some African Americans have rejected Christianity altogether and turned to Islamic or Muslim beliefs. Taking a more moderate position, other black churches have distanced themselves from the integration stance of Martin Luther King, Jr. and now advocate an exclusionary black church.

On the other hand, there is another exciting movement in African-American culture seeking to revive the preaching-style known as "narrative preaching." Sermons in this genre retell the biblical story in such a way as to bring it to life again. When the story is told, the preacher brings together the biblical world and the contemporary world. As a result, a universal theme is experienced, and a currently oppressed people can experience help from the same God who saved the oppressed in Egypt.

Although our postmodern culture wants us to quit telling the universal biblical story, we must realize that our culture cannot survive without a story, without the true story. Christians need to learn this story more fully and be able to tell it better. To "receive" Jesus, as Paul told the Colossians to do, meant much more than accepting a religion in your own personalized and individualistic way. No, it was receiving a very old message that was the hope of the ages and passed on not only to make a convert but also to save the world. We still need to sing the old song, "Tell me the old, old story of Jesus and his love."

Questions for Discussion

1. What is a metanarrative?

2. Read Colossians 2:6-7. What did Paul have in mind when he talked about "receiving Jesus"? How do we usually interpret this phrase?

3. What is the basic metanarrative or story of modernism? Why has it been rejected?

4. How has the metanarrative of modernism been seen as having produced exclusivism and violence? Give some examples. Do you agree with this assessment? Why or why not?

5. What are some of the "small stories" that have become acceptable in our culture?

6. Where can you find examples of sound bytes and aphorisms being used to replace metanarratives?

7. Give some biblical examples teaching that God's message is neither exclusive nor violent.

8. How can a positive metanarrative be proclaimed in our postmodern culture?

9. What would need to change for Christians to "receive Christ" as Paul teaches in Colossians?

7

Not Yet

Robert Duvall was robbed. I still can't believe he didn't win an Oscar for his portrayal of a Pentecostal preacher in the movie *The Apostle*. My only consolation is that he had already received an Oscar. I probably would have given him an Academy Award for his bit part as Boo Radley in the classic, *To Kill A Mockingbird*. But his Academy Award came for his unlikely role in *Tender Mercies*.

In *Tender Mercies*, Duvall plays a former country and western singer who, when his singing career is ruined by alcoholism, winds up working at a run-down motel for a widow and her young son. Eventually Duvall's character marries the widow and tries to drastically change his life. Demonstrating the transformation, both the young son and his new stepfather are baptized on the same day.[1]

As they drive home in their old pickup truck, the son reflects on their mutually shared experience and says to his stepfather, "Everyone said I would feel like a changed person. I guess I do feel a little different but not a whole lot different. Do you?"

"Not yet," Duvall replies.

"You don't look any different. You think I look any different?" asks the stepson.

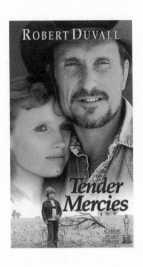

"Not yet."

According to the son's observation, "something was supposed to happen" at his baptism. But did it? Given his youth and inexperience, he wasn't sure. In this touching scene, it is almost as if he needed someone to tell him what had happened. The problem was that his stepfather, even though he was anticipating something happening, didn't know what had happened either.

The Modern Church

The church in Colossae was going through the same experience. They had all been baptized but they didn't understand it. They knew something had happened but they needed somebody to explain it to them. This is where Paul the apostle entered.

Studying the historical shifts in our society, we looked at modernism and said that it failed because it didn't deliver. Certainly science, technology and the accumulation of wealth will continue in our future. But we will no longer believe that any of these will bring ultimate knowledge, power or happiness. The real failure of modernism is that with modern man (or "self") at the foundation of society, it is not possible to figure out everything. Paul's warning to the Colossian church is worth repeating: "See to it that no one takes you captive through hollow and deceptive philosophy, which depends on human tradition and the basic principles of this world rather than on Christ" (Col. 2:8). Again, this is why Christians should not be overly influenced by postmodernism.

Not only has society been failed by the modern world but also by the modern church. As the modern period ends, the church reflects some of the same problems as the culture. Just how has the modern church failed Christians and non-Christians alike? The church itself started to act as if it had everything figured out. This was manifested in the attitude that through self-effort Christians could grow a church. Correct doctrine could be established with enough personal reasoning. Moral character and even righteousness were sought too often through self-effort. The source of knowledge, power and purpose in the modern church was frequently determined by "self." Self-determination, self-discipline, self-help, and personal leadership became the shifting sand foundation of many churches.

But Paul never thought that human beings could realize the fullness of Christ on their own efforts or insight. Notice what Paul says: "Entering into this fullness is not something you figure out or achieve" (Col. 2:10, MSG). The ultimate religion, according to the apostle, is not something you can fully grasp, let alone achieve.

One trait of modernism is that we, as a society, tried to figure everything out. In the church of my heritage, we tried to figure out everything it took to be the right church. We thought it was up to us to discover how to restore God's work and be the church of the New Testament. It was called "Restorationism." But too often we put the emphasis on our work of discovering the ancient pattern rather than God's revelation of his current movement.

During this modernist period people also began to doubt God's text. Some Christians even began to wonder whether God was big enough to deliver his whole message to us. As a result we again tried to figure out this dilemma by ourselves. Some began "demythologizing" God's word. Instead of restoring the church, demythologizers were restoring the text. But who became the ultimate source of what was myth and what was revelation? Again, it was man himself.

Since science could explain everything, the modern tendency was to dismiss the holy or supernatural. Mystery or anything that we could not explain by our own rationality was skeptically denied or ignored. In modern society we only believed things that we could see, prove or explain.

Modernism, as we came to know it, could almost be defined as "achievement through self." And self achievement didn't escape the modern church. We tried to show how good we were. We tried to show how much we had done. We tried to show how big we had grown. The goal of the modern church was to achieve success. If it became successful, we turned it into a formula and marketed it for repeated successes elsewhere. If churches today are not being seen as viable alternatives in the postmodern world, perhaps it is because they are rooted in the progress myth of success rather than in true spirituality.

In Colossae the culture of the age also got into the culture of the church. "It is not a matter of being circumcised or keeping a long list of laws. No, you are already in—insiders—not through some secretive initiation rite but rather through what Christ has already gone through for you" (Col. 2:11, MSG) The point is not "what you achieve" but what Christ has already achieved for you. Many now, as they were then, are trying to achieve something they already have. The philosophy of success through individual achievement simply didn't fit into Paul's theology to the Colossians.

As our culture has seen the failure of modernism in building a better world, many Christians have also seen the failure of the modern church in building a better relationship with God. A self-achieving modern church fails even in the basic foundations of salvation. When asked, "Are you saved?" many modern church members cannot answer this question positively. So what do they do? They try to learn more, do something more or be a little bit better, rather than relying on "what Christ has already gone through for you."

Paul says we have salvation. Do we, or is it "not yet"? Certainly salvation is a future hope as we look for the second coming of Jesus and our heavenly home. But it is also a present experience because of the grace in which we stand. However, Paul is most concerned here with salvation as a past event. Did something happen in the past that marks our redemption? Can we point to an event that signifies our salvation? If a sign or some assurance is needed, Paul gives some comforting words, "If it's an initiation ritual you're after, you've already been through it by submitting to baptism" (Col. 2:12, MSG). If Robert Duvall's character in *Tender Mercies* would have co-starred with the Apostle Paul, or at least read the correct script, he could have answered his stepson's searchings as Paul did, "If you are looking for rituals, you have one. If you want something to do, you already did it."

A Rite That's Not Wrong

Duvall's character didn't quite get it. The Colossians just didn't get it. And similarly, in our postmodern search for religious rituals and mystery, we must not lose sight of the basic rituals that God has prescribed for us as Christians. "Going under the water was a burial of your old life; coming up out of it was a resurrection, God raising you from the dead as he did Christ. When you were stuck in your old sin-dead life, you were incapable of responding to God. God brought you alive—right along with Christ!" (Col. 2:11-12, MSG).

In baptism there is a death. In this basic Christian ritual the old self dies. Not just our selfish living, but the whole system of a world built upon "self." As for knowledge, power and happiness, our baptism is saying, "I can't do it myself. I die to achieving these goals on my own. I am raised to a new life." It is through Jesus that God supplies us with knowledge, power and real happiness.

In baptism we are saying, in essence, "I am saved, because I am in Christ Jesus." Paul put it this way to the churches in Galatia: "For all of you who were baptized into Christ have clothed yourselves with Christ" (Gal. 3:27). Baptism isn't a work, it is faith. It is a receiving of what God wants to give you. It marks the revelation that "I will not have my 'self' at the foundation of my world any longer."

In the novel *A Day No Pigs Would Die*, a matronly aunt disciplines her young nephew because of his bad grammar. She tells him that if he were a fearing Baptist, he would do better in English. The frightened lad thinks to himself, "That was it! That there was the time my heart almost stopped. I'd heard about Baptists from Jacob

Henry's mother. According to her, Baptists were a strange lot. They put you in water to see how holy you were. Then they ducked you under the water three times. Didn't matter a whit if you could swim or not. If you didn't come up, you got dead and your mortal soul went to hell. But if you did come up, it was even worse. You had to be a Baptist."2

We have a lot of preconceived ideas of baptism. Many rational (and irrational) reasons are given for not practicing baptism. But in a postmodern age where people are looking for mystery and spiritual ritual, isn't baptism not only a good spiritual sign but also a ritual that proclaims the failure of self as a foundation?

The doctrine and practice of baptism needs a second chance in many churches. Indeed, baptism isn't bad. And neither is getting rid of your "self" as a foundation of your belief system. "Think of it! All sins forgiven, the slate wiped clean, that old arrest warrant canceled and nailed to Christ's Cross. He stripped all the spiritual tyrants in the universe of their sham authority at the Cross and marched them naked through the streets" (Col. 2:13-14, MSG).

Think of what Christ has already done for you.

Is he going to do something? If you are still saying "Not yet," look again: "All sins forgiven." Look again: "the slate wiped clean." Look again: "that old arrest warrant canceled" (Col. 2:13-14, MSG).

Not yet? Yes, yet. It has already happened.

As we enter the postmodern era, let us not preach a modern gospel focusing on all that we still have to do. Rather, let us preach about all that Jesus Christ has already done. Let's not convert to a church that is going somewhere. But let us convert to Christ who has already been to the grave and back. We need Jesus—no more, no less.

Questions for Discussion

1. What is supposed to happen at baptism?

2. Read Colossians 2:10. Where have you tried to figure out or achieve something rather than rely on the fullness of Christ?

3. Describe the difference in having a religion based on self-achievement as opposed to what Christ has done. Read Colossians 2:11.

4. If you were asked, "Are you saved?" how would you answer the question? What would be the basis for your answer?

5. Are rituals important in Christianity? If so, which ones? Read Colossians 2:12.

6. Why has baptism been divisive in churches rather than unifying? Should this doctrine be given a "second chance"?

7. Do you view salvation as "not yet" or something that has already been done? Explain.

8

Angels We Have Seen On TV

They're Everywhere

"Do you know a good book on angels?" was the question I was asked a decade ago. All I could recall was *Angels* by Billy Graham. I told my friend that if she went to the local Christian bookstore she could probably find Billy's book if she asked the sales clerk. If not, they could order it. Surely it was still in print.

It is a different matter now. How many new books have been written on the subject of angels in just the past few years? When Frank Peretti wrote his blockbuster thriller, *This Present Darkness*, Christians began serious interest in the subject of angels. Today if you want a book on angels you don't even have to go to a religious bookstore. Just stroll into any Walden Books or surf through Barnes and Noble on the web and you will see whole sections on angels. Literally hundreds of books are available on this heavenly subject; many of them are bestsellers.

If you look around, you will notice that celestial beings are not just in bookstores. If you want angels, just turn on the TV, and there is Monica in "Touched by an Angel." It was interesting to watch this show establish itself on the mainstream, secular entertainment schedule. It understandably started out very obscurely. I can imagine some tower-dwelling studio executive asking, "Who would watch a show about angels?" Similar shows had failed in the past specifically because they were "too spiritual." Even the television audience rating services seemed to verify that in our postmodern age most people would probably not be interested in a primetime television series based on the subject. It almost seems miraculous in itself that "Touched By An Angel" has become one of the most-watched shows on television.

And now we see angels on the big screen. Movie stars are reaping huge box office rewards acting in angelic roles. John Travolta's grungy portrayal of the archangel Michael in the movie of the same name proved to be a humorous story that successfully brought the subject of angels to the mainstream movie-going audience. Travolta's flawed angel acts more like Cupid as he attempts to bring two star-crossed lovers together using some rough and ready angelic tricks. He even raises a dog from the dead along the way.

The stars of "Touched by an Angel" (used by permission of MTM Studios)

Why are angels so popular again? Because we are living in a postmodern era. Indeed, we are coming to realize that science and technology cannot solve all our problems. The guarded good news of postmodernism is that postmodernists have a tremendous desire for spirituality. Television producer Aaron Spelling, who gave us such titillating shows as "Charlie's Angels," "Melrose Place" and "Beverly Hills 90210," said in regard to spirituality, "It is a huge awakening! A huge awakening! And I think we are going to see more of it instead of less." As a result, he produced a show called "7th Heaven." Why? "It is the show I want to watch with my kids. It's a show that Ron Howard [the director] wants to watch with his kids. It reminds you of the old Andy Griffith [shows]."

Theologian Robert Nash, Jr. says, "People have grown tired of the modern world with its extreme confidence in the power of science and human reason. They want something more—something that gives meaning to life. They no longer are attracted to rational arguments for the existence of God. They have discovered Mother Earth, crystals, star gazing, speaking in tongues, the Goddess, spiritual rebirth, ancient Native American emergence mythologies, and sacred places. In short, they have rediscovered faith."[1]

During the old era of modernism, "faith" was not valid in and of itself. Faith was only as valid as the reasoning behind it. But today we are becoming aware of the true validity of faith. If there is anything good to come out of postmodernism, it may be the rebirth of faith itself.

But again Nash foretells the bad news of our postmodern age. "If the good news is that spirituality has been reborn, the bad news is that the rebirth has happened outside the walls of the church."[2] And it is this issue that touches on another possible explanation as to why angels have become so popular.

Nora Ephron, the writer and director of John Travolta's movie, "Michael," explains: "What people can't stand is, everyone wants to believe God notices you, that He notices the details . . . The horrible truth is that He probably doesn't notice. He's got more important things to do. But angels do notice. You know, they make the tow truck come when you have a flat tire."[3] As a result, in our postmodern society, angels seem to be better than God. At least they seem more universal and somehow more personal.

Nothing New Under the Son

The writer of the book of Hebrews also had to deal with the attraction to angels in competition with deity:

3 The Son is the radiance of God's glory and the exact representation of his being, sustaining all things by his powerful word. After he had provided purification for sins, he sat down at the right hand of the Majesty in heaven.

4 So he became as much superior to the angels as the name he has inherited is superior to theirs. (Hebrews 1:3-4)

The place and rank of angels compared to Jesus was not only a first-century problem but has also surfaced to an even greater extent in our postmodern age. New Testament commentator David Garland states, "Another thing that makes angels so attractive today is that they are non-denominational—transcending creed, religion and philosophy. They offer generic, inspirational stuff with little or no religious content." As a result, postmodern-day angels have become popular because they are not necessarily tied to any specific denomination nor are they the sole property of any one religion. They are perceived as just being spiritual. Garland further states that, "Angels give us what we want without demanding much religious commitment or sacrifice in return."[4] It's almost as if God comes with too much baggage, so many postmodernists would rather have an angel.

The Apostle Paul also encountered this problem in the church at Colossae. In that day, just as today, a large spiritual movement was developing. This movement resulted in all kinds of religious elements. It is hard to say if it started within Judaism or whether it arose from an outside source. But the emphasis was focused on fasting, religious rituals, holidays and, yes, even angels. The biblical text points out Paul's admonition to the Colossians:

16 Therefore do not let anyone judge you by what you eat or drink, or with regard to a religious festival, a New Moon celebration or a Sabbath day.

17 These are a shadow of the things that were to come; the reality, however, is found in Christ.

18 Do not let anyone who delights in false humility and the worship of angels disqualify you for the prize. Such a person goes into great detail about what he has seen, and his unspiritual mind puffs him up with idle notions. (Colossians 2:16-18)

The church in Colossae had become very spiritual but, as Paul points out, there was a serious problem. The Colossian believers had emphasized the rituals and the angels but not the meaning behind it all. Spiritual and religious things are okay, but only if based in truth and reality. The Colossians had missed the reality of Jesus.

Today's emphasis on angels usually stops short of the reality of Jesus. You hear about angels, religion, spirituality and even God in current movies and television shows concerning angels—but seldom about Jesus. As Paul notes in Colossians 2:19, "He has lost connection with the Head, from whom the whole body, supported and held together by its ligaments and sinews, grows as God causes it to grow." And like the first-century Colossians, we have the same problem in postmodern society. For all their spiritual interest and seeking, postmoderns have lost connection with Christ as the Head.

In Romans Paul deals further with this matter using the celebration of holidays as his focus: "He who regards one day as special, does so to the Lord. He who eats meat, eats to the Lord, for he gives thanks to God; and he who abstains, does so to the Lord and gives thanks to God" (Rom. 14:6). The message is clear. If we are going to celebrate a holiday, like Christmas, we must celebrate it for Jesus. Most people celebrate Christmas in all ways but remembering Jesus.

I have even heard some say that they only celebrate Christmas in a secular way since the Bible doesn't specifically mention the holiday. Paul gives freedom for holidays. But he says that our holidays or "special" days should be done "to the Lord." If holidays, rituals or angels don't get connected to the ultimate reality of Jesus, then they have no purpose for Christians.

The bottom line is that rituals, holidays and angels are all fine as long as we maintain our focus on the truth behind them. There are certain specific issues which must be prioritized in order to maintain proper focus. For instance, Jesus himself warned against meaningless repetition in prayer: "But when ye pray, use not vain repetitions, as the heathen do: for they think that they shall be heard for their much speaking" (Matt. 6:7, KJV).

Even holy events like the Lord's Supper lose their significance if they are simply repeated in a meaningless manner. No event relates more to Jesus than the communion meal. And yet few events promote more cliches and mindless participation than this meal of thanksgiving. Many Christians either don't practice it anymore or do so infrequently. The key is not to lose the ritual but to somehow make the reality of the event a meaningful experience.

But the Colossians took the rituals one step further. Instead of letting them be events to unite believers, they used one's celebration or lack of it as a means of judgment. In fact, they became downright competitive in their religious observations. "Therefore do not let anyone judge you by what you eat or drink, or with regard to a religious festival, a New Moon celebration or a Sabbath day" (Col. 2:16).

"I fast—you don't!" "I don't need to celebrate Christmas—you do!" "I believe in guardian angels—you don't!" When fringe areas of faith become the focus of our message, we make the same mistake the Colossians made. The peripheral areas of our beliefs should lead us to the heart of the gospel not away from it. Not all spiritual matters are as important as others. But whatever we do in our postmodern society, it must be related to Jesus. "And whatever you do, whether in word or deed, do it all in the name of the Lord Jesus, giving thanks to God the Father through him" (Col. 3:17).

The Biggest Religious Story of the Century

As mentioned earlier postmoderns are open to spirituality and are even seeking it. But what is meant by spirituality? In defining spirituality, Robert Nash, Jr. says, "The church often understands 'spirituality' to be the appearance of certain kinds of activities—specifically, morning devotions, worship attendance, or Bible studies. But spirituality is properly defined as the creation and cultivation of an intimate relationship with God. It is actually a state of being or a relationship that is based, not upon activity, but upon intimacy."[5]

The widespread seeking of spirituality among postmoderns should be good news for the church. But it may not be a happy ending for many congregations. In their quest for spiritual experience postmoderns are looking outside the church because, believe it or not, it is harder and harder to find spirituality within the church today. As noted by Christian analyst Mike Regele, "Thousands of churches are about to die. That's right! The number one religious story of the next century will be the deaths of thousands of local Christian churches. These churches will die slow and painful deaths brought on by changing demographics and their unwillingness to face the reality of their own spiritual inadequacy." Regele goes on to state, "A local church has only two options as its surrounding culture moves from modernity to postmodernity. It can die because of its resistance to change or it can die in order to be reborn as something new. Either way, the church as we know it will die. Most churches are choosing the first alternative. The second choice is possible only if old structures and approaches and perspectives give way to new ones."[6]

Postmodern people can be reached today with the gospel of Jesus. However, many congregations are not going to do it. If we miss the mission, it will not be because the culture wasn't open to faith and spirituality.

To reach postmodern seekers today, we must have meaningful spiritual ritual. And to be the church, the meaning, the spirituality, as well as the ritual, must be tied directly to Jesus. No more, no less.

Questions for Discussion

1. Do you hear more about angels today than in the past? Give some examples.

2. Why do you think angels are so popular today?

3. Read Hebrews 1:3-4. Do you think angels are more popular than Jesus in a postmodern world? Why or why not?

4. Read Colossians 2:16-18. How had the focus of faith shifted off Jesus in Paul's day? Do you see similarities today? Where?

5. How can spirituality and religion not be based on truth and reality?

6. Read Colossians 1:19. What does it mean for faith to be connected to the head, Jesus Christ?

7. What are some examples of religious rituals that have been disconnected from Jesus?

8. Why does it appear that many of today's churches will die in the near future?

9. Describe "meaningful, spiritual ritual" for the church in our current culture.

9

The Philosophers Have Taken Over the Asylum

I received my salvation by the grace of God. I received my master's degree by the grace of Dr. John Eggleton. Let me explain.

To obtain a master's degree in religion at Eastern New Mexico University, I had to be found formally proficient in several fields of study. It was like proving to the university graduate faculty that you had the equivalent knowledge of someone who had graduated with a major in these specific fields of expertise. In addition, the Religion faculty could ask you any question they wanted within these fields, whether it was Old Testament, New Testament, or any other chosen field.

Now the real art of passing master's level oral examinations is to have the right professors examine you. At least you try to stay away from those dreaded professors who wouldn't think twice about reducing your grey matter to mush. So when they gave me a choice of being examined in Greek or philosophy, I chose philosophy. To tell you the truth, I was afraid because someone told me that the Greek professor was a cross between John Houseman's crusty, old law professor character in the movie "Paper Chase" and "Atilla the Hun" in such an exam. As it turned out, I probably should have chosen to take my chances with Greek.

I had taken some undergraduate courses in philosophy and figured I could pull some all-nighters before my orals to "philosophize" my way through the exam. As God would have it, this ended up being quite a dumb move. I had forgotten how challenging the subject of philosophy was and how much there actually was to philosophize about.

When the day of my oral examination arrived, the religion department had chosen Dr. John Eggleton to handle the philosophy questions. Dr. Eggleton was not your ordinary, run-of-the-mill philosophy professor. No, he was the distinguished head of the entire philosophy department. It wasn't a pretty picture when he started asking questions.

During a break in the festivities, as I was attempting to fight off a panic attack of major proportions, Dr. Eggleton casually came over to me and whispered, "You don't know this stuff, do you?"

I took what I thought was going to be my last breath as a master's degree candidate and whispered back, "No sir."

As the gravity in the room began to pull all the color from my face, he smiled forgivingly and said, "If you get through this, will you promise me you will study philosophy more?"

"Oh, yes sir!" I replied, hoping my knees weren't making too much noise for him to hear my whispered response.

Years later when Dr. Eggleton died, he was considered by many to be one of the top scholars in both the Old Testament and the field of philosophy. And, please, if any of you make it to heaven before I do, will you tell him that I'm continuing to do my penance by writing this book on postmodernism?

I thank God for Dr. Eggleton. Through his grace and prodding, I started my quest to understand not only philosophy but also this new philosophy of postmodernism. I have now come to understand that the study of philosophy is essential if one is going to grasp the real "thought" behind our worldviews. Philosophy becomes the foundation for all that we do. Unfortunately, at times, even a bad philosophy can become popular. That was the case in Colossae. And it seems to be happening again today in our postmodern era.

An Idiot's Guide To Philosophy

For those of you who haven't studied philosophy and wouldn't like to take an oral exam from the head of a philosophy department, let me simplify the whole field of study. Philosophy revolves around three major disciplines. Each discipline has a technical name, so let me introduce each one by asking a rhetorical question. Then I will discuss the problem posed by postmodernism in each of these disciplines.

1. What is real? (Metaphysics)

We first have to decide what is real. Am I real? Is God real? Is evil real? This is the question of "being." As noted in the book of Acts, "For in him we live, and move, and have our being; as certain also of your own poets have said, For we are also his offspring" (Acts 17:28, KJV).

According to Paul, reality for Christians is rooted deeply in the revelation of Jesus Christ. Jesus is our metaphysical answer. He defines reality for us. We may not be eyewitnesses to the facts of his story. But from the text of the Bible, we believe that we can establish a reality based on Jesus. As we previously saw in Colossians, "These are a shadow of the things that were to come; the reality, however, is found in Christ" (Col. 2:17).

In postmodernism truth has been individualized to the point that there is no definitive, final truth. The postmodernist says, "You have your truth and I have mine." As a result, reality itself becomes personalized. With the exclusion of any metanarrative or overall story to explain things, we eliminate the necessary path to a universal reality.

2. How Do I Know? (Epistemology)

Once we declare reality, the logical question is "How do you know?"

In postmodernism there is a distrust of the "science" and the "reasoning" that for the previous modern society was the source of knowledge. As we saw in a previous chapter, Christians would answer the epistemological question of "How do I know?" with the simple words of the old song, "Jesus loves me this I know, for the Bible tells me so." This answer might seem quite reasonable, but it is complicated by the postmodern belief in "deconstruction." If words have no solid reality as deconstructionists believe, how can knowledge be obtained from a book?

The concept of deconstruction is difficult to understand because its roots go back to a French philosophy which is next to impossible to understand. For ease of discussion, let's use the recent presidential impeachment trial of Bill Clinton as a stark public example of deconstruction. The key issue to understand is this: If there is no truth, then it is impossible to lie. Words, in effect, lose their weight and reality.

If language is arbitrary and personal, then how can anyone be guilty of perjury? Do you remember the testimony? The President denied having "sexual relations" with "that woman." But in later testimony it came out that he had his own interpretation of what "sexual relations" meant. As a result, during the impeachment trial the President's highly paid defenders jumped on the band wagon and deconstructed the term "sexual relations" to show that it has no fixed or solid meaning, only an array of conflicting interpretations. They asked, in effect, how can one commit perjury when all you have is conflicting interpretations about the meaning of words?

When Mr. Clinton was asked if he was ever "alone" with Ms. Lewinsky, he said, "It depends on what you mean by being alone." Most people would interpret this as being alone in the same room with Ms. Lewinsky. But he reasoned that it could be interpreted that he was never alone because other people were in the White House. This postmodern case is a grand example of how words are a matter of one's own perspective. If this is true, how can words be the basis for knowing the truth?

This philosophical stance is a problem for Bible believers. We believe that some words are "God breathed" giving us a definitive source for knowledge.

3. How do I live? What is moral? (Axiology)

The Christian's biggest problem with postmodernism may lie here. If there are no absolutes, if words don't count, how do we find a solid basis for morality? How can we really judge correctly in an impeachment trial—or in any dispute, for that matter? If we remove the metanarrative and say that there are no universal truths, that everyone can have their own little story with their own personal truth, how do we judge right from wrong? If all the diverse stories are okay and of equal value, who are we to judge anyone, even if their personal story is guided by the worldview of an Adolph Hitler?

The funny thing is, we all seem to "know" instinctively when something is wrong. But the problem with postmodernism is that we can't "articulate" it anymore. In reality, society needs someone to stand up and say when something is wrong. Some elements of our postmodern society (i.e., our schools and government) seem to have difficulty dealing with those bold enough to make such truthful statements.

This is what happened to a Christian father who confronted the principal of a local school in Washington state which sent home a flyer with a list of New Age rules for students. The document included such statements as, "You can have anything you want" and "There are no rights and wrongs." The parent pointed out that if these statements were true, it would not be wrong for a kid to bring a gun to school and kill someone. This parent pointed out the ludicrous nature of these rules many years before the Littleton, Colorado tragedy and others like it. This is where meaningless rules like these can lead.

How did we end up with tragedies like the one at Columbine High School? It is much more complicated than blaming a school, a parent or even a non-conforming peer group. In 1976 Francis

Schaeffer wrote his important book, *How Should We Then Live?* whose title is based on the passage where Ezekiel is called to be a watchman for the people. "Therefore, O thou son of man, speak unto the house of Israel; Thus ye speak, saying, If our transgressions and our sins be upon us, and we pine away in them, how should we then live?" (Ezek. 33:10, KJV). Or to say it another way, "Now as for you, son of man, say to the house of Israel, 'Thus you have spoken, saying, "Surely our transgressions and our sins are upon us, and we are rotting away in them; how then can we survive?"'" (Ezek. 33:10, NAS95).

Schaeffer talks about the basis of American civil law: "Certainly we aren't a Christian nation but the founders based it [the law] on some Christian principles, believing that God gave us a law to live by and that people who obey it will be better off. This was based on the philosophy of Samuel Rutherford called 'Lex Rex.' In other words, 'the law is king.'"[1] Lex Rex (law is king) means that there is a definitive law that governs the behavior and the actions of any king or government. Rex Lex (the king is law) means that a ruler or ruling body can determine the law without a definitive basis for the system of justice.

Schaeffer declared decades ago that as a society, we were moving rapidly away from Rutherford's concept of Lex Rex, and that the law itself would eventually be its own justification. Schaeffer further stated, "In the United States many other practical problems developed as man's desire to be autonomous from God's revelation—in the Bible and through Christ—increasingly reached its natural conclusions. Sociologically, law is king (Samuel Rutherford's Lex Rex) was no longer the base whereby one could be ruled by law rather than the arbitrary judgments of men and whereby there could be wide freedoms without chaos. Any ways in which the system is still working is largely due to the sheer inertia of the continuation of the past principles. But this borrowing cannot go on forever."[2]

Supreme Court Justice Oliver Wendell Holmes, Jr. put it this way: "Truth is the majority vote of that nation that could lick all others. So when it comes to the development of a corpus juris the ultimate question is what do the dominant forces of the community want and do they want it hard enough to disregard whatever inhibitions may stand in the way."[3] To extrapolate from Justice Holmes' wise observation, it is easy to see why President Clinton wasn't removed from office during his impeachment trial. As a society, we didn't want him to be.

This concept of "dominant community forces" is, of course, very different from that of "Lex Rex." Today our postmodern society makes decisions based on what is sociologically helpful at the moment. But what does this tell us about the future? It may be that we will find ourselves without any actual basis for morals.

As the Governor of Colorado said in his comments on the youthful gunmen's manner of dress and anti-social behavior at Columbine High School, "So many people knew this was wrong but no one could say it. Were we just afraid that we would hurt the self esteem of these kids if we said it was wrong?"

How should we then live? We can't live this way. At least, not for long. You can't drive a car in a postmodern way. Can you imagine it? There must be some rules of the road which are absolute. Ultimately, a philosophy with no rules simply breaks down for everyone.

The End Of It All

The Holy Book does tell us how to live. It reminds us that there is, indeed, a right and a wrong way to live. Eugene Peterson in *The Message* renders the Apostle Paul's admonition to the church at Colossae in this way: "So if you're serious about living this new resurrection life with Christ, act like it. Pursue the things over which Christ presides. Don't shuffle along, eyes to the ground, absorbed with the things right in front of you. Look up, and be alert to what is going on around Christ—that's where the action is. See things from his perspective.

"Your old life is dead. Your new life, which is your real life— even though invisible to spectators—is with Christ in God. He is

your life. When Christ (your real life, remember) shows up again on this earth, you'll show up, too—the real you, the glorious you. Meanwhile, be content with obscurity, like Christ.

"And that means killing off everything connected with that way of death: sexual promiscuity, impurity, lust, doing whatever you feel like whenever you feel like it, and grabbing whatever attracts your fancy. That's a life shaped by things and feelings instead of by God. It's because of this kind of thing that God is about to explode in anger. It wasn't long ago that you were doing all that stuff and not knowing any better. But you know better now, so make sure it's all gone for good: bad temper, irritability, meanness, profanity, dirty talk.

"Don't lie to one another. You're done with that old life. It's like a filthy set of ill-fitting clothes you've stripped off and put in the fire. Now you're dressed in a new wardrobe. Every item of your new way of life is custom-made by the Creator, with his label on it. All the old fashions are now obsolete. Words like Jewish and non-Jewish, religious and irreligious, insider and outsider, uncivilized and uncouth, slave and free, mean nothing. From now on everyone is defined by Christ, everyone is included in Christ.

"So, chosen by God for this new life of love, dress in the wardrobe God picked out for you: compassion, kindness, humility, quiet strength, discipline. Be even-tempered, content with second place, quick to forgive an offense. Forgive as quickly and completely as the Master forgave you. And regardless of what else you put on, wear love. It's your basic, all-purpose garment. Never be without it" (Col. 3:1-15, MSG).

What does Colossians say here? There are rights and wrongs. If the Colossians didn't get them in their philosophy-gone-wrong world, Paul spelled them out.

Even if the postmodern world doesn't want to hear the truth, we must tell it to them anyway. Why? They are living in a world that they know is not working. Everyone knows that something is wrong.

Listening to my least favorite radio announcer in Seattle the other day, I heard a most unlikely message. In reflecting on violence in schools, this postmodern, anti-Christian announcer stated, "The only thing I have heard recently that makes any sense came from a minister. I'm so desperate for an answer I'm listening to a minister."

If we truly have answers to the biggest philosophical questions of the day, how can Christians be quiet? Talk radio stations are full of people calling in and asking, "What is wrong?" We have the answer. We can't retreat. Christians must engage the postmodern mind. Believers need to keep telling the truth. Indeed, we have good solid answers to the three biggest philosophical questions.

As I mentioned earlier in this book, the father of postmodernism was Frederick Nietzsche. When Francis Schaeffer reflected on the philosophy of Nietzche even before the days of postmodernism, he made a prophetic critique: "Modern people and modern theology, in trying to start from man alone, are left where the brilliant German philosopher Friedrich Nietzsche (1844-1900) found himself. Nietzsche in the 1880s was the first one who said in the modern way that God is dead, and he understood well where people end up when they say this. If God is dead, then everything for which God gives an answer and meaning is dead.

"I am convinced that when Nietzsche came to Switzerland and went insane, it was not because of venereal disease, though he did have this disease. Rather, it was because he understood that insanity was the only philosophic answer if the infinite-personal God does not exist."[4]

According to Schaeffer the logical conclusion for a postmodern philosophy is insanity. If a person says, "I don't know what is real. And I don't know how to know anything. And I have no way of distinguishing right from wrong," what would we conclude? Put him on the stand in a courtroom. What would be the verdict? We would judge him insane.

Is a philosophy that ultimately can't answer the basic questions of reality, knowledge or morals any better?

Questions For Discussion

1. How do people decide what is "real" today? Read Colossians 2:17. How does Paul define reality?

2. Where do people turn for a source of knowledge in our world today? Where do Christians go to find a basis for knowledge?

3. What are some examples of deconstruction? Why are words still important in Christianity?

4. What has become the basis for morals in our postmodern world? How does this differ from a Christian position?

5. What is the difference between Rex Lex and Lex Rex? How has the post-modern world evolved into a "king is law" viewpoint?

6. Read Colossians 3:1-15. How does Paul distinguish between right and wrong?

7. How has postmodernity left us with a philosophy that has the makings of madness?

10

This Is My Story, This Is My Song

Bastian went to the bookstore and acquired the strangest of books. The bookstore owner told him that he now possessed a different kind of book. It did not contain a typical story. If he read it, he would get caught up and absorbed in its drama. It was not only a book that brought life, but it was also a book in which Bastian would live. In fact, Bastian would actually become a part of the life of the very book itself.

Like Bastian's book in *The NeverEnding Story*, the Bible is a Book of Life—but it is so much more than that. As we read it, we are caught up in its drama. The story of the people in the Word becomes our story. It is a book in which we live.

Narrative Evangelism

In the previous chapter, we looked at deconstruction and how words don't seem to have a reality anymore. The flip side of this issue is that words connected into a narrative may be one of the most effective ways to communicate or to discern a reality.

Kevin Graham Ford, in his pivotal book on evangelism, *Jesus For a New Generation*, says that one of the most powerful methods to reach postmoderns is "narrative evangelism."[1] "As our culture increasingly moves away from logic- and proposition-oriented thought forms and deeper into feelings-oriented and trans-rationally-oriented thought forms," Ford says, "the only evangelism that speaks the language of the culture is a story-oriented evangelism. Narrative evangelism speaks the language of a media-saturated, story-hungry generation. It gives people a point of connection in their everyday lives, enabling them to see how God has interacted with human history and how he can interact with their own individual lives."[2]

Being able to tell the story is perhaps the best way to reach our current postmodern world. Since everyone in the postmodern era wants to tell their own little story, the reverse is also true—that nearly everyone will listen to your own story (even if it is part of a metanarrative).

According to Ford, "Narrative evangelism begins with the story of God's interaction with human history and with individual human lives. It is the story of how God sent his son into the world—and how he invades and revolutionizes an individual human life. . . . It leads to a vision of one's own story as a subplot of a grand and inspiring story."[3]

In postmodernism we have shifted from the large stories of the metanarratives to small stories of the individual. Everybody has a right to her or his own story in a postmodern world. But as Christians, we believe we have more than just another small story. Paul states in his theme for the book of Romans that there is a unique and dynamic power connected to our story. "I am not ashamed of the gospel, because it is the power of God for the salvation of everyone who believes: first for the Jew, then for the Gentile" (Rom. 1:16). And this particular story not only has power connected to it, but it also produces faith as it is proclaimed, making it different from an ordinary story: "So then faith cometh by hearing, and hearing by the word of God" (Rom. 10:17, KJV).

In our culture today the facts are not enough to convince. In fact, they may not even be heard coherently by the masses. Without a story there is little chance for belief.

In the O. J. Simpson murder trial the main issue was just this— the facts versus the story. Prosecutors Marcia Clark and Christopher Darden presented overwhelming facts, but it seems that the case was lost because they were never able to tell a believable story of how O. J. could have committed the crimes.

In the modern age people tended to argue about words. If the words were rational and conclusive, belief was born. But in the post-modern age apologetics revolves around story. Faith is born when the story is believable and transforming. As a result, effective Christian witness must revolve around the telling of our dynamic story. And in order to gain a hearing as a viable alternative to the smaller narratives of the day, it must be told convincingly.

If you saw the TV miniseries, "Noah," it probably bothered you. It did me. The obvious flaw was that they didn't tell the story right. But the interesting issue is, Why did this bother me? Why did I care so much? The answer is because it is my story. As the old hymn proclaimed, "This is my story, this is my song."

And why didn't NBC care enough to do it right? It wasn't their story.

Consider the perspective of story as Moses remarks to the nation: "Hear, O Israel, the decrees and the laws I declare in your hearing today. Learn them and be sure to follow them. The LORD our God made a covenant with us at Horeb. It was not with our fathers that the LORD made this covenant, but with us, with all of us who are alive here today. The LORD spoke to you face to face out of the fire on the mountain" (Deut. 5:1-4).

Is this story true? Were these people to whom Moses was speaking present when the story took place? Were they actually face to face with God as Moses proclaims? Were these the actual people at Horeb? No, the eyewitnesses had already died out. But Moses, as the story teller, uses first person narrative to let them know that it is their story too. They live in this story just as we all live in God's "Never Ending Story."

Fred Craddock, the great teacher of preachers, tells the story of a young boy who knew his ethnic origin. He was Native American. He could check that as a category on an application form. He could even recite some facts about "Indians" in general. But one day he met a Kiowa tribal leader and had the opportunity to sit down and be with him all day. That day he heard the real stories of his people. When he left that day he no longer just knew about the Kiowa, he *was* a Kiowa. Their story was now his story.

It is the story that makes us who we are. And until we hear our own story not even our own lives make sense. We discover the truth about who we are as we become a part of the story.

Experiencing The Story

Modern and postmodern people see stories differently. Modern people tend to analyze stories. Postmodern people want to experience stories.

This is a tough cultural change for many Christians. In premodern times mystery was accepted and valid. Therefore faith itself was valid. But in the modern age mystery was lost. Everything could be figured out through scientific method. When the mystery was lost, so was the validity of the story. Modern man simply resorted to analyzing the message to show that it was true. But with the death of the progress myth, story has once again taken the day away from analytical reasoning.

This cultural change shouldn't really bother Christians. The Bible itself notes that Jesus was quite a story-teller: "With many stories like these, he presented his message to them, fitting the stories to their experience and maturity. He was never without a story when he spoke. When he was alone with his disciples, he went over everything, sorting out the tangles, untying the knots" (Mark 4:33-34, MSG).

In the philosophical mess that existed in first-century Colossae, a similar solution was needed. What was the church to do? Paul's admonition centers on story. "Let the word of Christ—the Message—have the run of the house. Give it plenty of room in your lives. Instruct and direct one another using good common sense. And sing, sing your hearts out to God!" (Col. 3:16, MSG).

Paul's solution was twofold: teach the story and sing the story. Again, Paul's premodern advice well suits the postmodern age well.

(1) Teach the Story. In other words, "words" still have solid meaning to Christians. And our faith is not devoid of a story. We have always been the people of a story. And the story has personal meaning, because we have experienced it. The key is this—you don't have to prove the story or analyze it to death—just tell it. Faith comes by hearing. But the story must be told more than analytically. It must be revealed experientially. The heart of the testimony must tell how the story crosses our path of existence and has become our own personal story. And the mystery of the message must be disclosed—this personal story can become everyone else's story as well. The story must be told in order for it to become their story.

(2) Sing the Story. Our story is to be sung with everything that we have in us. We don't sing it to analyze the story. No, we sing the story to experience God through the song. "[P]ostmodern worship must be something altogether different. It must celebrate the joy of life in Christ. It must be centered in the retelling of the Story in such a way that the worshipers find themselves inside the Story even as they worship. Pre-postmodern (or modern) worshipers sat on the outside looking into the Story. They analyzed the story—its characters, its plot, its plausibility. Postmodern worshipers want to sit inside the Story itself. They want to embrace it and live it," says author Robert Nash, Jr.[4]

Every time we have had a revival of Christian faith in a culture, there has been an outpouring of new songs. And nothing reveals a cultural clash and shift more than music. Is anything more controversial in churches today than music and worship styles? A cappella or instrumental, traditional or contemporary, praise teams or worship leaders, drums or drumless, guitar or organ—we all want different things from our spiritual music because all of us experience the music differently. Why? Because we all want it to be our own song.

Again, it is like the words to that old hymn, "This is my story, this is my song." If it isn't our song, it's hard to connect with it.

Paul qualifies the teaching and singing that he is prescribing to the Colossian church. In Colossae there is "bad philosophy." In other words, people love wisdom that is wrong. In Colossians 3:16 Paul is turning the church to loving godly wisdom which he defines as having "the word of Christ richly dwelling in you." As a result, a wise church does more than communicate words. It reveals the story of a life which has Jesus richly dwelling in it.

Similarly, worship should stem from the "thanksgiving" of one's own soul. Our song, according to Paul, should be rooted in a personal thankfulness that should be reflected in all our being. Karl Barth tells the story of someone who sees people in a front yard looking up at the sky. The man does not know what is in the sky. He does not know what is up there—is it good or bad? His only clue is to look at the expressions on the people's faces. Barth's point is that our very faces and our lives are an apologetic to the God who is up there. All some people initially will see is our countenance. From our expressions, what will people think is up there? Will they think God is good, bad or indifferent? As a result, we sing with thanksgiving revealing the very nature of our God.

Recently I observed two videos for children. The first was one of the most professionally done animated stories of David and Goliath that I have ever seen. The story was correct. The cartooning was breathtaking. The music was suspenseful. I couldn't think of a better way to tell people the great story of the little boy who slew the giant, until . . .

I saw a video done in a Sunday School class in Nashville. There was no animation. No professional actors were a part of this video. The music lacked great intensity. But it was much better than the first one. Why? The children of the Sunday School class were the actors.

I'm assuming that the Sunday School teacher was the giant. The whole story was acted out in the most hilarious fashion imaginable. The kids put their own stamp on the story. But more importantly, they were inside the story. It was now their story. Is there a better way to teach postmodern children?

As God rescued David and the Israelites from Goliath, he has rescued me from the giants of my life. Robert Nash, Jr. states it this way: "The Bible must become a source of life-changing stories that all emerge from a single great story and that individually assist human beings in living inside the Story.

"The focus in a postmodern world must be upon participating in the story that rests at the heart of the Bible. In the modern world, the stories of David and Goliath, of the Creation, of Paul's shipwrecks, of Jesus and the woman with the hemorrhage, led us to ask, 'How can I defend these stories against those who don't believe them?' The burden of proof rested on the church's shoulders.

"Today we should ask a different question. 'How should I live in light of these stories?' The stories then become the shaping influence upon our lives and the evidence of their truth resides not in scientific proof, but rather in the fact that Christians pattern their lives by them."[5]

"This is my story, this is my song, praising my Savior all the day long."

Questions For Discussion

1. Why is "story" so important in a postmodern age?

2. If you were to tell your story, what are some of the key elements you would include in it?

3. Why does a postmodern person want more than facts?

4. What is different about the Christian story when compared to other stories?

5. Read Colossians 3:16. What are some good ways to communicate our story today?

6. What is the difference in talking about a story and being in a story?

7. How can Christians help people to live inside the story of the gospel?

The Purpose-Driven Life

"There's no use going anywhere to preach unless you preach everywhere you go."—St. Francis

What an indicting statement! The church goers and clergy of St. Francis' day were convicted. Francis was admonishing people who go great distances to take the message of Jesus but never tell anyone at home. It's still a good admonition. Why would we send people around the world to tell others about Jesus if we don't tell our neighbors about Him in our own backyard?

St. Francis is teaching us not to compartmentalize our religion. Faith should not be limited to certain places or times. We should encourage people to talk naturally about Jesus wherever they are, not just at church. We all should be putting in a good word for Jesus wherever we go.

If you understand this idea, you will understand the Apostle Paul's teachings to the Colossians in chapter three. Paul now moves from ideology to practicality. He has already stated that there is a bad philosophy in the land. And he notes that we need "Christ—no more, no less" as a basic theology. But Paul realizes that we still have to live our lives. How do we live in a world that has sold out to a bad philosophy? Answering this practical question, Paul gives us the secret, a "funnel" through which everything in our lives should pass.

Relational Thinking

As a professor of homiletics (preaching), I always have my students begin sermon preparation by writing out the focus statement of their sermon. The students must condense the theme or idea of their sermon down to a single, meaningful sentence. And this is exactly what Paul is now doing. He is trying to give the Colossians a focus statement for their lives. In this focus statement, Paul reduces everything down to one sentence on how a Christian should live in a world built on a bad philosophy. Paul's focus statement is this: "And whatever you do, whether in word or deed, do it all in the name of the Lord Jesus, giving thanks to God the Father through him" (Col. 3:17). That's it. It's pretty simple, and not a bad way to live one's life.

As we look at our society today, we see a unique brand of purposelessness. At a seminar I once attended, "postmodernism" was defined as "existentialism gone to seed." But this may not be that helpful since it is more difficult to define existentialism than postmodernism.

Maybe the best way to understand existentialism is to watch a Woody Allen movie. One of my favorite Woody Allen lines comes from his Oscar-winning movie, "Annie Hall": "A man goes to a psychiatrist on behalf of a friend. He says, 'My friend fancies himself a chicken.'

'Why don't you bring him in for treatment?' says the psychiatrist. 'Oh, I would, but we need the eggs!'"

Allen is saying that the world in which we live is absurd. There is no metanarrative or overall purpose to give it sense. People don't really relate to one another—but we still need the relationships. There is no meaning or reason for our relationships, but life is not as valuable without them. And since there is no reason or meaning for the universe, we simply fill our lives with meaningless relationships. It doesn't make sense, but we still need the eggs.

In a postmodern world, without an ultimate purpose, how do we know what to do? Are we to be led by our feelings (I need the eggs)? Should we be led by chance like pinballs? You know which direction a pinball goes, don't you? Its direction is totally determined by what last bumped it. Which direction do postmoderns go? It usually depends on what, or who, last bumped them—a spouse, a boss, a church. . . .

What Paul is boldly saying is that our direction should be set by our purpose. I call this concept "relational thinking vs. terminal thinking."[1] Relational thinking is the process of relating activities and knowledge to a specific objective. Terminal thinking is the process whereby our activities and knowledge are ends within themselves. In other words a terminal thinker becomes programmed by his or her activities and relationships. He just goes to a movie, watches TV, eats out, majors in this, moves here. It is the "Nike" philosophy—"Just Do It." Activities and people govern our lives rather than an overall purpose. So we just stay busy "doing it." The problem of postmodernism in general is not that the end justifies the means, it is that without an end, any means is fine.

In relational thinking you relate what you are doing to your objective. What do you do? Where do you go? Whom do you spend time with? These questions are answered by a purpose. If an activity can be related to an ultimate objective, then it will be seen as a good thing to do. If it can't be related, then you don't do it.

What then is a good ultimate objective? Isaiah stated one: "Everyone who is called by my name, whom I created for my glory, whom I formed and made" (Isa. 43:7). In this passage we find our primary reason for existence. The very reason we were created is to glorify God. As a result, a relational thinker asks questions of his life in reference to whether it glorifies God or not. Does this activity glorify God? Would another activity glorify God more? How can this relationship glorify God? The answers to these questions determine the direction of the relational thinker.

Jesus also had a relational purpose. He stated, "For the Son of Man came to seek and to save what was lost" (Lk. 19:10). Jesus related what he did and with whom he spent his time to his objective of the salvation of people.

Accountants For Christ

Relating everything to the purpose of glorifying God may seem easy if you work for a church like I do. But what about people who work in the "real world"? Let me tell you about my friend Dennis Dodson. Dennis is an accountant for Christ. I know a lot of accountants but few accountants for Christ.

Dennis and I went to school together at Texas Tech. He studied accounting there. When I moved to Seattle to start a campus ministry at the University of Washington, he moved with me. He told me that since he was an accountant, he could get a job anywhere. Therefore he would take an accounting job during the day and help me do campus ministry at night. He related having a job in accounting to a greater purpose of glorifying God through telling college students about Christ.

By the time he got to Seattle and took a job downtown, Dennis' car had broken down. As a result, Dennis had to ride the bus to work every day. Not to be discouraged, he related his bus ride to his objective of leading people to Jesus. Many times as I would ask people in our campus ministry how they happened to come, they would tell of a man on a bus who invited them. A man who was more than an accountant—an accountant for Christ.

One Sunday morning a young lady walked to the front of the church to give her life to Christ. I asked her who she was. She replied, "I am Dennis Dodson's secretary." Again, he was an accountant for Christ.

But being an accountant for Christ is more than simply inviting people to the Lord. It is doing your job as for the Lord. It is keeping accurate books. It is being on time and working hard during the whole day. It means not cutting corners but handling all the numbers with absolute integrity. Dennis was an accountant but so much more. He related every aspect of his occupation to his purpose of glorifying God.

Many think, "I can't do much for the Lord with my job. If only I had another type of occupation, then I could serve the Lord." It is not the particular occupation that makes a job holy. It is whether you relate your job to your purpose.

Relational thinking involves more than jobs. What do you do with your leisure time? Does it relate? I love to play golf. But you can golf or you can golf for Jesus. What is the difference? Do you relate the golf to your purpose? What is golf anyway? It's a long walk. I have realized that I cannot take a walk with anyone for four hours without bringing up the Lord at some point in time. However, most golfers don't talk much about Jesus (at least not in context). But most golfers are not golfers for Christ.

One of my fondest memories in life was when my good friend John Tholl told me on hole number 14 at Jefferson Park Golf Course that he wanted to give his life to the Lord. In the course of the round, a natural conversation had developed that brought Jesus into the reality of a couple of friends' lives.

I'm not saying that I don't play golf to score well or even to win. But I just try not to forget my purpose when I'm on the links.

Most of the time as a Christian it is not what you do or don't do. It is not that you are with this person as opposed to another—it is whether your actions relate to your heavenly purpose. It all depends on whether you relate your situation to your purpose. This is how Christians are to live in a postmodern world— with great purpose!

A church recently asked me to address what they considered to be the three biggest problems in Christianity today. The first problem was a lack of evangelism. In other words, we were not leading many people to the Lord. The second problem was what was called poor retention. In other words, most of the people who came to the Lord were falling away and not becoming committed disciples. The third problem was that we were also losing our children who were raised in the church. As they got older they also were dropping out.

As I considered all three of these problems, I found that they had a common root. All of them were centered in a lack of being able to talk about Jesus in natural situations. In other words, Christians were not relating faith to the ordinary situations of life where people best learned. We were not being evangelistic because we weren't naturally talking to the unchurched and relating Jesus to their lives. We were losing people at church because we weren't talking about Jesus to new Christians in natural situations. We were trying to formalize the teaching and it became ineffective. Our children were falling away because we didn't talk to the kids naturally around the house. The activities of our home simply didn't relate much to Jesus. In other words, our biggest church problems could be traced back to a lack of relational thinking.

Jesus gives the example of a purpose-driven life in the way he trained his disciples. He didn't have to create a school. His school was wherever he found himself. If he saw a sower in the field, he related it to the kingdom. If a storm came up on the Sea of Galilee, what a good opportunity to teach faith. If people were hungry, what a great time to feed them. Jesus related everything in his life to his purpose of seeking and saving the lost. It didn't matter where he went because he preached everywhere he was.

If there is one needed factor to reach postmoderns today, it is authenticity. If faith cannot be lived in natural settings and in real world situations, Christians will be quickly sized up as phonies. If Christians must resort to canned approaches or only bringing people to their own turf, the message will not be accepted. Authentic Christianity will be faith that is expressed in everything we say or do. Whether it is our message or our action, it will relate to Christ—nothing more, nothing less.

Questions For Discussion

1. How do Christians compartmentalize their religion?

2. Can you think of some good examples of existential living in our postmodern world?

3. What is relational thinking? What is terminal thinking? Which one of these best describes how you live your life?

4. Read Colossians 3:17. How does Paul paint a picture of relational thinking?

5. What purposes should drive the life of a Christian?

6. What are some specific ways that you could relate your job and activities to your purpose for living?

7. How is a lack of relational thinking related to the most common problems in the life of the church?

8. How was Jesus a relational thinker?

9. What would an "authentic" Christian look like to you?

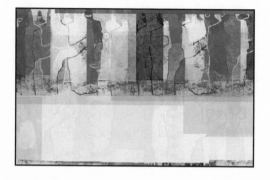

12

Where Can You Go When the World Won't Treat You Right?

Last year three million youth were infected with the HIV virus. The Center for Disease Control and Prevention's "National Center for Health" not only released this alarming statistic, but also a conclusion even more shocking. The study states that the "one thing" parents can do to decrease the chances of their children being infected with a sexually transmitted disease, having casual sex, being raped or becoming divorced is to "stay married." No, this wasn't a preacher or a counselor talking. It was the Center for Disease Control.

Anchor Your Family

Postmodernism has not produced a stable environment for families. Perhaps it is because postmoderns desire to upgrade everything. With our computers the same old thing is never good enough. We feel that we have to upgrade constantly to remain functional. Of course, we do the same thing with our cars, houses, clothes—and now we are even doing it with spouses. As author David Garland notes, "The problem is that when marriage partners get caught in the vortex of thinking, 'My needs must be met first,' neither have their needs met. The result is divorce, particularly if we have bought into the modern marketing mantra that we should continually upgrade to new and improved versions. The incalculable damage to children and our family and community is considered less important than the pain in the relationship. We have become too devoted to ideas of self-assertion and self-fulfillment to appreciate the concept of servanthood and its very different joys. We may be afraid to trust our happiness to anyone else, so we keep our unconditional commitments to ourselves."[1]

What's wrong with today's family? This is the question that is being asked more and more in our postmodern society, especially since the shootings at Columbine High School. Nowhere can the results of the lack of absolutes, the tolerance of everything, and the removal of metanarratives (the big stories of truth) be seen more than in the break up of the family. The question has been asked over and over, "Shouldn't a parent know if his kid is making bombs in his own home?"

Again in Colossians, Paul gives the following advice that could be very helpful to our current family dilemmas: "Wives, understand and support your husbands by submitting to them in ways that honor the Master. Husbands, go all out in love for your wives. Don't take advantage of them. Children, do what your parents tell you. This delights the Master no end. Parents, don't come down too hard on your children or you'll crush their spirits" (Col. 3:18-21, MSG).

In a sentence, Paul is saying: "If society is going adrift, anchor your family."

Commenting on this passage in Colossians, David Garland states, "The home becomes even more important as the center of Christian nurture and education when surrounding society becomes so wicked that it accepts and even promotes immorality. These texts are not about who gets the power and authority to run the family but affirm that the family is the primary context for faith formation and for living out one's faith. How we live in our family says a great deal about our faith."[2]

How do we stabilize an unstable world? First of all, we need godly families to survive the instability of our society. Just like the theme song from the popular television show "Seventh Heaven" asks, "Where can you go when the world won't treat you right? The answer is home."

A transformation of society will require more than good families—it will take godly families. In Leo Tolstoy's famous novel *Anna Karenina*, which deals with adultery, Tolstoy notes, "All happy families are more or less like one another; every unhappy family is unhappy in its own particular way." Tolstoy is saying that you can go wrong in a lot of different ways but there is typically only one way to do something right.

In reality there hasn't been more than one way to have a good family. The supreme guidelines for good family relations are all set forth in the Bible. What God has to say about family may seem a little outdated or old fashioned by today's standards, but it still works. Certainly there are exceptions, but for the most part, Christian families are great families. The biblical guidelines still work, even today.

What can Christians do to give a positive alternative to post-modernism? Few things will be more effective than keeping their families together—but this may not be enough.

Even though Christians can present to the culture an example of healthy family life, more will be needed to heal the current fractured relationships in today's homes. The solution is more than godly families. Godly churches must also minister to families who have not practiced godly principles. We need godly churches to substitute for ungodly families.

Too many people in this postmodern world don't have a good answer when you ask the question, "Where can you go when the world won't treat you right?" Their answer is not "home." The family has frequently been the problem not the solution in their lives.

Intergenerational Reconciliation

One of the difficulties of the "family movement" in evangelicalism over the last couple of decades has been its lack of outreach to those outside the church. At times the family has taken precedence over the mission of God. As a result, people have pulled away from churches to do their own "family thing." This of course is not the answer. Certainly we need to have good families, but our families must also form a community in the church for those who do not come from good families and are presently hurting because of their home life.

When an actual "revival" happened on the University of Washington campus a couple of years ago, it was interesting to note the substance of the college students' testimonies. The common thread in their stories was a coming to the Lord from a position of hurt or suffering. There was not a story told that didn't include the pain of a broken home. Too often, instead of having a parent helping them when they were children, they had to be like parents themselves to their selfish parents. In such a society the church must become a surrogate family.

In a culture full of broken families, Jesus' alarming teaching on family takes on special relevance: "Whoever does God's will is my brother and sister and mother" (Mk. 3:35).

At an Ivy Jungle conference on university churches, a particular campus ministry was singled out as the most effective in the country. When their campus minister, Mike Gaffney, was asked to tell what he considered the most important aspect of his ministry, he responded, "Connecting generations together."

Gaffney went on to say that most college students today have never had a significant, deep and meaningful relationship with a person of an older or younger generation. He perceived his job as a mission to bring these generations together. Whether it's getting older folks to adopt younger people or just having different generations of people meet together, it should be the mission of the church. These cross-generational interactions are what is missing in today's society.

As so many churches are doing more and more to separate age groups, healing ministries have seen the need to get the generations back together.

Deep inside, young people from broken homes are longing for this contact even if they don't know it. In fact, this may be at the heart of the noted inner suffering of Generation X. Too many of the younger people today remain isolated in their own generation. If they do not experience meaningful multi-generational interaction, will they find the needed healing to their hurt? Emotional and spiritual healing may not take place until young people connect with someone of another generation.

Where is this generational interaction going to happen? Is there a better place than the church? Perhaps the church is the only place this can happen in our society. To reach a postmodern world, the church will have to become a healing community, a community of family, and a community of generational reconciliation. In a world of separation Christians will have to commit to being substitute fathers, mothers, children, grandparents and grandchildren.

With a postmodern emphasis on diversity, generation gaps have become acceptable rather than tragic. As the Christian message proclaims spiritual reconciliation, racial reconciliation and denominational reconciliation, generational reconciliation cannot be left behind. What can break down the walls of the ages? Christ—no more, no less.

Questions For Discussion

1. What are the biggest problems, as you see them, facing today's family?

2. Read Colossians 3:18. How can a family that is going adrift be anchored?

3. Why do Christians need to do more than stabilize their own families? How can we best help other families?

4. How would you define "intergenerational reconciliation"?

5. Can churches actually be a part of the process that separates generations? Explain. What are some practical ways that the church can connect generations?

6. Have you noticed the suffering of Generation X that is caused by the lack of relationships with other generations? Can this generation be whole or healed without this reconciliation? Why or why not?

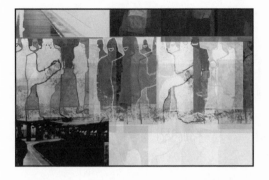

13

We're All Going Somewhere

A Metro transit bus traveling through the University District in Seattle had two different advertising panels on its side. One ad was for the Open Door Baptist Church and it read, "We're all going somewhere . . ." On the other panel was an ad for Metro transit system which read, "Relax. There's more than one way to get there." Does anything better picture our dilemma? Christians insist that we are going somewhere (heaven—but only through Jesus). The rest of the world, hating the exclusivity of our claims, simply resolves to relax and go whichever way they want.

How do you evangelize a culture where nothing would seem more wrong than the evangelization of a culture? As Christians we are going to have to decide either to remain aloof and let everyone do their own thing because that is what they want us to do or to engage our culture with a different message because God wants us to do it.

Paul certainly wanted the Colossians to engage their culture when he wrote, "Be wise in the way you act towards outsiders; make the most of every opportunity. Let your conversation be always full of grace, seasoned with salt, so that you may know how to answer everyone" (Col. 4:5-6). Being wise and knowledgeable are imperative in Paul's estimation if a Christian is to reach non-Christians in their own culture. Paul's advice calls the Colossians to be like the men of Issachar "who understood the times and knew what Israel should do" (1 Chron. 12:32).

Urie Bender in his descriptive book on evangelism in the modern era, *The Witness*, described ministry with a focus on the message, the mission, the motivation and the method.[1] The essence of his analysis is that the message is the gospel; the mission is the world; the motivation is love; and the method is making disciples. These descriptions are certainly true in any culture. But in postmodern culture certain emphases are particularly appropriate.

The Message

In a postmodern world the "message" better be a message of grace. When Paul approached his philosophy-gone-bad culture, he taught the same: "Let your conversation be always full of grace." To understand our times is to realize that a legalistic message won't work as it did in modernity. A purely legalistic message is always wrong, but in certain times and places it can become popular. In areas like Galatia, legalism became popular and grew despite its false doctrine. But this kind of message is not going to work today. A blessing of postmodernism is that it will create a culture unresponsive to legalistic, works-oriented churches. Seeing the failure of self-help in modernism will prepare postmoderns to see the reality of the failure of self-righteousness.

The message for a postmodern culture is grace. Placing grace at the center today is important for a specific reason. Postmodern society says that all stories should have the same weight and that there is more than one way to get to the truth. If this is the claim, then we, as Christians in postmodern culture, need to show how all stories are not the same. Indeed, we must demonstrate that not every way leads to the truth.

When it comes to showing the differences between stories, the biggest difference between the Christian message and others is the element of grace. No other doctrine better distinguishes Christianity from other religions. Christianity is the only world religion that is not works-oriented. Only the gospel of Jesus Christ offers salvation not based upon merit. In a culture that has already recognized the fallacy of getting better and better, grace truly can be seen not only as a fresh point of view but also as truly good news.

But with Paul grace is more than the message. The message is to be given with graciousness. Perhaps it will be this unique graciousness seen in relationships that will break down the walls of animosity toward the exclusive message of the gospel. Graciousness can overcome the misgivings and misunderstandings between people. Perhaps Christians today can leave behind the cocky arrogance that often marked churches in the modern era. Finding a gracious way to tell the story of grace will be the key to opening the seemingly closed doors of postmodernism.

Graciousness is not the only mark of the message. Paul also says that it is to be "salty." In our idiom that might sound like it's full of profanities. But in the first century, "seasoned with salt" meant witty, amusing, clever or humorous. In other words, the Colossians were to make sure that they were not ignored simply because they had become irrelevant bores.

Recently I was told that the greatest expectation for non-Christians when they go to church is that it will be boring. Too often that has been true. The message of the gospel is anything but boring. How tragic that it appears boring! In a fast-paced, easily bored society, it is crucial—now more than ever—to tell the message in an exciting and enthusiastic manner.

The Mission

Why aren't churches evangelistic today? There's an easy answer. We are not reaching young people. In his 1990 work *Signs of the Times*, Paul Tans revealed the incredible statistic that in America

95% of believers become Christians before they reach the age of 25.[2] And the ages of conversion seem to be getting even lower. In *Closing the Back Door*, Thom Ranier reveals that 82% of the believers in the United States came to Christ before the age of 20, and that 74% became Christians between the ages of 9 and 14.[3]

If evangelism is going to take place in our postmodern culture, it will have to happen with young people. People in our Western society tend to get locked into worldviews at a very early age. As open-minded and tolerant as our culture claims to be, Americans seem to stick with their early beliefs, good or bad.

Since today's society is doing everything it can to get its postmodern worldviews fully engrained into our children well before the age of 14, Christians are also going to have to get the message of grace out to today's youth. If it doesn't happen before the age of 14, we risk losing future generations.

Change has been extremely difficult for churches as the modern world has given way to the postmodern. However, churches that are interested in evangelism will do more than change for the sake of change. They will have to change for the sake of the mission. They will have to change in order to help younger people find Christ.

Paul pointed out to the church at Colossae that, even though their story was true, they must be wise in how they present it. His advice may be even more important in a postmodern cultural shift. Older church members accustomed to modern thought and modern churches will be reluctant to change. But that reluctance may thwart the church from accomplishing its mission.

The Motivation

One of our problems as Christians is that we may have spent too much energy maintaining our umbrage against postmodernism. Our approach has been that we are right and they are wrong. Such an inflexible tactic in dealing with those of another viewpoint doesn't work well in our current age of tolerance. Christians who actually want to see change should not react in a hostile way to postmodern people. Perhaps it would be more helpful if our motivation came from the realization that postmoderns are not only wrong but also suffering because of it.

Tom Beaudoin, in *Virtual Faith*, describes the characteristic that he believes best marks the younger generations of today. While some say that our youth are whining, he believes that, as a group, they are indeed suffering.[4] Of course, if we knew someone was suffering, our approach to that person would be quite different. With emotional hurt involved, an evangelistic encounter certainly demands more than the discussion of what's right and wrong. Surely this rings true regarding how we would deal with our own children. A good parent seeks to discern whether his child is complaining or truly hurting. In the same way, if we approach people with this same discernment, we will see doors open not only through sensitivity but also through the ministry of healing past wounds.

The Methods

Kevin Graham Ford, in his book *Jesus For a New Generation*, spells out three methods of evangelism which best reach the postmodern world.[5] First is what he calls "Process Evangelism." Process in evangelism means that Christians need ways of telling the good news over a long period of time. One shot approaches and quick questionaires are not going to work with postmoderns as they did in the modern age. Essentially, the postmodern mind needs to examine the authenticity of the stories that they hear. They will not take things at face value even if a good presentation of the facts is made. If an evangelistic approach is over after one shot, then a non-Christian will not have an opportunity to evaluate the character of the Christian sharing his faith. A Christian's authenticity over the long haul will usually be critical in the process of conversion.

As a result Christians must model the message. They must be able to talk about the gospel over a long period of time if authentic faith is to be demonstrated. Certainly this is not inconsistent with what Jesus did with disciples. He walked with them for three years.

He lived with them. And the future apostles were able to see and feel the authenticity of his story.

In a postmodern age modern methods of outreach must be re-evaluated. Not only do five-fingered exercises and four spiritual laws diminish the capacity for authenticity, they also teach in a linear thought process that is quickly receding in postmodernism. Young people grasp information quickly but not usually in a step-by-step method. Have you ever watched young kids learn a new video game? They don't read the instructions. They don't go consecutively from level to level. They simply grasp large sections of information through their experience in the order that moves them at the moment. The gospel will not be taught to postmoderns according to the order we want to share it as much as in the order they want to learn it.

Indeed, leading someone to Christ will be a relational process in a postmodern age. During the 90s we saw the shift away from the effectiveness of planned programs of evangelism. *Christianity Today's* research on evangelism found that natural evangelism was 57% more effective than a "canned approach." To be effective in the future, Christians will have to learn to talk naturally about Jesus in everyday life situations.

The next method of evangelism noted by Ford is the "Embodied Apologetic" approach. With this method the Christian himself becomes the best argument for Christianity. Embodied apologetics is more a way of living than a logically constructed argument like we have seen in the popular approaches of Josh McDowell or Francis Schaeffer in the waning years of modernism. When Christians become "authentic people" the postmodern person will take note. Therefore, the real question for the immediate future is not, "Can Christians prove what they believe?" but rather, "Can Christians live what they believe?"

To illustrate this point, postmodern analyst Stanley Grenz says, "If you step into the pulpit and you say, 'I'm going to give you five reasons to believe in God,' and the reasons you give are all intellectual, evidential and cosmological, you'll have little or no impact. The impact comes when you can say with authenticity, 'I've been knocked around by life, but through the pain of it all I've experienced that God is there.' That's an embodied apologetic, and that counts with Thirteeners (Generation X)."

Ford's third method of evangelism is the "Narrative." This is where you tell "The Story" by telling "your story." You share with others your own personal testimony. Everybody has a story. But as Christians we believe that ours is true.

Again Kevin Graham Ford states: "As our culture increasingly moves away from 'logic' and 'proposition' oriented thought forms and deeper into 'feelings' oriented and 'trans-rationally' oriented ways of thinking, the only evangelism which speaks the language of our culture is a 'story-oriented evangelism.' Narrative evangelism speaks the language of a media-saturated, story-hungry generation. It gives people a point of connection with their everyday lives, enabling them to see how God has interacted with human history and how he can interact with their own individual lives."[6]

Illustrating the point that everybody has a unique story that needs to be told, Fred Craddock tells of eating with his wife at the Blackberry Inn in the Great Smokey Mountains of Tennessee. As they relaxed looking out a big picture window, a very old man came to the table and introduced himself. When the crusty old fellow found out that Fred was a preacher, he said, "Let me tell you a story." Then, the old man proceeded to do just that.

"I was born in these mountains. My mother wasn't married. In those days that was the greatest shame a person could carry. When we went to town, the people would look at me and then at her, and I could tell they were trying to guess who my father was. It was painful and humiliating. I felt like nothing. At school kids made fun of me and called me all kinds of bad names. I hid. I ate alone.

"When I was 9 or 10, I started going to a church at a place called Laurel Springs. There was a preacher there. A cranky rough sort. He had a bushy beard and a big voice. He scared me to death and fascinated me at the same time. I came late and left early so no one would say, 'What is a boy like you doing in church?' or 'Who is your daddy, anyway?'

"One Sunday they had an altar call and I couldn't get out like I usually did. I panicked. I knew someone would stop me and expose me and ask me about my father. Suddenly there was a big hand on my shoulder. I looked up and it was the preacher. I was terrified.

"Then he said it. 'Boy ... Boy, you are a child of . . . Boy, you are a child of . . . God. . . And I see a striking resemblance.' Then he swatted me on the bottom and said, 'Go claim your inheritance.'"

As the old man paused, Craddock said, "What's your name?"

"Ben. Ben Hooper," was his casual reply.

Craddock thought for a moment about the story he had just heard, and then he said, "I remember my dad told me that the people of Tennessee twice elected a man named Ben Hooper as governor. Would that be you?"

The old man slowly nodded his head and said, "Yes... I was born that day. . . in that church."

Questions For Discussion

1. Why is evangelism so unpopular with non-Christians today? . . . with Christians?

2. Read Colossians 4:5-6. What advice does Paul give for sharing our faith?

3. What part of our message needs to be emphasized in a postmodern world?

4. Why is it so important to reach young people today with the gospel? What difficulties does this present for the church?

5. When sharing the message of Jesus, what attitude and motivation must be present?

6. What is "process evangelism"? Does this style differ with what you have been taught in the past? Why is process important in postmodernism?

7. What is an "embodied apologetic"? What are some examples of this method of evangelism?

8. Give your testimony as an example of the power of narrative.

14

Bad News Radio

Bad news. Yes, all the news stories, as Barbie and I were driving to church Sunday morning, were sensational, alarming and just plain bad news. Barbie mumbled something to herself and turned off the steady stream of info-speak, bringing an eerie silence to our mini-van (the kids weren't with us).

With a few more minutes left before reaching the church building, I turned the radio back on and switched it to my old standby. "That's why I listen to sports radio," I said politely. Barbie rolled her eyes and looked out the window, letting me know that she would have preferred the silence. I tried to overcome her indifference with some well-placed enthusiasm. "No, really. This is the station with the good news. They talk about baseball, football, and golf! They give the scores. They name names. There is no such thing as a bad statistic, you know. It's all good stuff." Not impressed with my analytical stretch, Barbie switched the radio off again and closed her eyes to the morning sun. At that point, I got the hint—albeit a few minutes late.

As we continued in silence, the residual effect of this "teachable moment" began to sink into my brain—which was already stuffed with my sermon notes, what I didn't eat for breakfast and the details of driving the car. "Indeed," I thought to myself, "where is all the good news?

"Didn't someone out there, on this beautiful Sunday morning, do anything good? Certainly Sunday is a slow news day. But what about Saturday night? Something good must have happened last night somewhere in the world. At least on sports radio—Tiger Woods must have made a putt!" But even sports radio only talked about recent Seattle sports—more bad news.

Doesn't anyone have anything to say that is good anymore? In a nihilistic, postmodern world it is understandable that bad news rules. But did the conversation change when I got to church? That's the important question.

People Are Important
Leaving out the conclusion of Colossians might make sense. It's only a bunch of names. Yet maybe there is something there in all those salutations that is still worth examining.

My major professor in graduate school, Dr. Stephen Eckstein, always told me, "If God let a passage survive, then there must be a reason." Then why is it there? Surely it isn't as important as some of the other sections. But maybe it still has a lesson for us. Let's see if we can find it.

7 Tychicus will tell you all the news about me. He is a dear brother, a faithful minister and fellow-servant in the Lord.

8 I am sending him to you for the express purpose that you may know about our circumstances and that he may encourage your hearts.

9 He is coming with Onesimus, our faithful and dear brother, who is one of you. They will tell you everything that is happening here.

10 My fellow-prisoner Aristarchus sends you his greetings, as does Mark, the cousin of Barnabas. (You have received instructions about him; if he comes to you, welcome him.)

11 Jesus, who is called Justus, also sends greetings. These are the only Jews among my fellow-workers for the kingdom of God, and they have proved a comfort to me.

12 Epaphras, who is one of you and a servant of Christ Jesus, sends greetings. He is always wrestling in prayer for you, that you may stand firm in all the will of God, mature and fully assured.

13 I vouch for him that he is working hard for you and for those at Laodicea and Hierapolis.

14 Our dear friend Luke, the doctor, and Demas send greetings.

15 Give my greetings to the brothers at Laodicea, and to Nympha and the church in her house.

16 After this letter has been read to you, see that it is also read in the church of the Laodiceans and that you in turn read the letter from Laodicea.

17 Tell Archippus: "See to it that you complete the work you have received in the Lord."

18 I, Paul, write this greeting in my own hand. Remember my chains. Grace be with you. (Colossians 4:7-18)

Colossians doesn't end like Paul's other writings. In his Thessalonian correspondence, Paul doesn't mention names. In Galatians, Paul is more than a little bit upset, "Let no one cause me trouble—grace be with you." In his brief letter to Philemon, some of the same people listed in Colossians are mentioned, but not in as much detail. So why so much attention to Paul's faithful colleagues in such a short letter?

In Romans 16 Paul also gives a lengthy list of greetings. And the common thread between these two letters is that Paul hasn't been to either place. In these works of correspondence, Paul is making note of the individuals whom both he and his readers know personally. He is using this literary mechanism to find common ground with those he doesn't personally know.

But is there another reason that this type of correspondence is effective, a reason which also ties in with the major theme of Paul's book? Examine once more the theme statement: "See to it that no one takes you captive through hollow and deceptive philosophy, which depends on human tradition and the basic principles of this world rather than on Christ" (Col. 2:8). Perhaps Paul is indicating that "hollow and deceptive philosophy" produces a particular kind of problem where this type of salutation is especially helpful. If so, what is behind these salutations?

In the first place, Paul is letting his readers know that the work of ministry involves a network of Christians. In other words, neither he nor anyone else can do it alone. Additionally, he is letting his audience know that there are, indeed, other churches and other Christian believers on their side. Paul is able to see the Christian church as a large community made up of smaller parts. Therefore as Paul meets people and connects with fellow believers wherever he goes, he has expanded his view of the church. Paul's unique realization is that there are, indeed, many other Christians, but they are not all exactly alike.

This concept is essential for all Christians to understand. Since we are living in the postmodern global-world, we need to be farsighted enough to see beyond ourselves. Paul is pointing out to his readers that if you are part of a minority group, and not part of the currently popular worldview, you had better know who your friends are.

In the second place, Paul is pointing out in his letters that ministry involves a team of friends. Paul realizes he "needs" other people to be successful. He needs friends in other places (both high and low) and, additionally, he needs to have friends with him on his journeys (either personally present or interceding in prayer). He is convicted that other Christians have made him successful. And as a result, he has also made them successful. Luke and ultimately Mark are both examples of the symbiotic relationship of lifting each other up and making each other more effective.

Where Have All The Heroes Gone?

Paul is also teaching us that ministry involves saying good things about people, and mentioning them by name. Look at his lists:

Tychicus—dear brother, faithful minister, faithful servant, encourager. . .
Onesimus—faithful and dear brother. . .
Aristarchus—fellow prisoner. . .
Mark—welcome him. . .
Justus—fellow worker, a comfort to me. . .
Epaphras—servant, prayer warrior, hard worker. . .
Luke—dear friend. . .

Postmodernism has produced a negativism not only in our view of the world but also in our view of its people. Postmodernists tend to have a negative, irreverent spirit toward the church and even toward people in general. As Christians in a postmodern world, we easily have taken this negative attitude into our relationships at church.

Church is to be an "alternative," in the best sense of the word. It should be a place where "good" is said of people by name. Christians in a postmodern world should practice Paul's counsel to the Romans and "outdo one another in showing honor" (Rom. 12:10). In this world most people are put down lower and lower. In most worldly conversations, when someone is put down another usually tries to find something worse to say. In the church we should build each other up higher and higher. Paul says "outdo." This means if a good word is said about someone at church, then you are to say something better and try to outdo what was said previously. This doesn't mean that we should not rebuke sin when we see it. But as a general standard for communication, we should say good things when we are talking about people.

The author and journalist George Will in his book *Men At Work* offers an interesting observation about heroes: "We live in a relentless anti-heroic age. Perhaps in a democratic culture there always is a leveling impulse, a desire to cut down those who rise. Today, however, there also seems to be a small-minded, mean-spirited resentment of those who rise, a reluctance to give credit where it is due, a flinching from unstinting admiration, a desire to disbelieve in the rewarded virtue of the few. We have a swamp of journalism suited to such an age, a journalism infused with a corrosive, leveling spirit. . .

"It requires a certain largeness of spirit to give generous appreciation to large achievements. A society with a crabbed spirit and a cynical urge to discount and devalue will find that one day, when it needs to draw upon the reservoirs of excellence, the reservoirs have run dry. A society in which the capacity for warm appreciation of excellence atrophies will find that its capacity for excellence diminishes."[1]

As Will notes in this book on baseball, the broadcasts on the sports station as well as the news station are bad. They are demeaning. There are no heroes because everyone tries to bring everyone else down to a lower level. Paul, in contrast, not only doesn't practice this in his relationships, but he also sets a new standard for our communication. We are to say good things about people.

The church in the postmodern world should be the one place where you can still tune in and find the good news: about Jesus—about people—about life.

Questions For Discussion

1. What are some examples of the "bad news" you hear every day?

2. In the conversations you hear, are people usually "put down" or "lifted up"?

3. Read Colossians 4:7-18. What is unusual about this passage? What can you learn from these salutations?

4. Which people in your life are helping you to be more effective in living for Jesus?

5. How is Christianity a big, world-wide network?

6. Read Romans 12:10. Give an example of "outdoing one another in showing honor."

7. What has caused the disappearance of heroes in our world? Who should be acknowledged as heroes in our culture?

8. How can you be more of a conduit for "good news"?

15

Final Answer?

As I was eating at my favorite hamburger establishment, a young kid passed by me with what appeared to be a very annoying T-shirt. As he got closer to me I could read the front of his shirt. It said, "God is dead—Nietzsche." I was more than a little irritated until he sat in the booth across from me and I saw the back of his shirt. It read, "Nietzsche is dead—God." It was a pretty good lesson. When it comes to philosophy, God does have the final answer.

In our earlier discussion of postmodernism, we used the fall of the Tower of Babel as an illustration of the end of modernism. We compared the building of the Tower of Babel to the building of the modern world. It was as if the architects of the modern world constructed a tower to exalt human beings. As they built higher and higher, they envisioned the capacity to see things as God sees them. Through science, technology and the accumulation of wealth, the tower builders sought to erect a centralized and unified social culture. The message to the world was one of unparalleled progress.

But the carousel of progress has stopped. Modernity has fallen. The unified worldview of modernism has fragmented into global cultural confusion. Race against race. Country against country. Men and women vying for position. Generations opposed to one another. Churches competing against other churches.

The progress myth that was supposed to bring everyone together did not deliver. Instead of a single focus, we have been left with a kaleidoscope of cultures. The controlling philosophy birthed out of the Enlightenment is no longer dominant.

Postmodernism has been called a carnival. Modernism was more like a circus. In a postmodern world there is no longer a central focus that dominates as in a circus. In fact, there is not even the choice of a three-ring circus. Instead, we are left with a carnival reflecting a multiplicity of incongruous events.[1] The carnival crowd of postmodernism imitates well the chaotic wanderings of the crowd at the end of the fall of Babel. The people have lots of activity and diversity. But no one is really communicating to the majority of the people. No one is able to understand the voices of the other people.

What Caused Postmodernism?

How did we get to this point? We could conclude that postmodernism is the ultimate end of human arrogance. Although this is an accurate assessment, perhaps the real reason is greater and more complicated. Could the cultural pain and confusion be God's doing? Perhaps postmodernism is the judgment of God for modernity.

Genesis 11 tells the result of the fall of Babel: "Come, let us go down and confuse their language so they will not understand each other. So the LORD scattered them from there over all the earth, and they stopped building the city" (Gen. 11:7-8). Is it possible that the confusion and diversity of our postmodern world is a judgment similar to Babel where God confounded their speech and scattered the people in various directions?

It would be hard to argue with the opinion that the people of the modern West became the most arrogant people in the history of the world. How could God not bring judgment on such a people?

If postmodernism truly is the judgment of God, then we must ask: Is this the end or is there hope for the future of our culture? Certainly

there are final judgments, but if a culture still exists in any form it would seem that there is the possibility of repentance.

The end of Babel was the end of the tower, but was it truly the end of the tower builders? Didn't God provide a way out for the scattered people? The story of Babel doesn't really end with the fall of the tower. In fact, the story of Babel is only at the beginning of the metanarrative. The story continues from Babel to Abraham to the exodus to the monarchy to the exile and the return—and ultimately to Jesus. Yet even that is not the end of the story.

The Plot Resolves

Finally, at Pentecost with the beginning of the church we see some serious plot resolution in the story of the fall of Babel.[2]

The judgment against Babel was basically twofold. First, their language was confused to such an extent that they could no longer hear and understand each other anymore. Similarly, critics have rebuked modernism because of its refusal to listen to minor voices. All but the major metanarrative was ignored. Could it be that the multi-lingual voice of postmodernism exists primarily because of the failure of the dominant voice of modernism?

Second, the judgment against Babel resulted in the splintering and dispersing of the tower builders. While this was certainly a judgment in one sense, it also helped fulfill God's initial intent in creation—multiplying and filling the earth. As postmodern philosopher par excellence, Jacques Derrida, comments: "The story of Babel does not merely figure the irreducible multiplicity of tongues; it exhibits an incompletion, the impossibility of finishing, of totalizing."3

Both of these judgments are addressed again at Pentecost. When the Jews assembled for the great feast, they came from all over the world. The very people who had been scattered in the Jewish dispersion are now brought back to Jerusalem. God's chosen people, who for hundreds of years had lived all over the world with only a hope for the restoration of their past, are now together. The unifying promise that a blessing for all people would come from them seemed like a dream.

But on that day of Pentecost the dream came true. Resolution of the fall of Babel came in two areas. First, the people who had been scattered are now brought back together to become a people of community. A new fellowship, a oneness is created in the new spiritual dimension of the church.

Second, the Holy Spirit, who is poured out at Pentecost, opens the ears so that all can hear. Babel resulted in confusion of speech where no one could understand. Pentecost resulted in the miracle of everyone being able to hear in their own language. Unity is not achieved by human efforts but by the power of the Holy Spirit.

The critiques of modernism have been based on the belief that Western society has been blind and deaf to other cultures. The metanarrative of modernism has left out certain people groups, especially the oppressed and poor. Postmodernism preaches that all of these stories need to be told. But telling the many stories still doesn't solve the problems of oppression or poverty, much less redemption. The telling of stories and the sensitivity to others' journeys may be needed, gracious and helpful—but it is not enough. It can bring acceptance of diversity, but it doesn't bring reconciliation. The greatest problems are not solved without reconciliation. Reconciliation takes place when these diverse and scattered people can find relationship with each other. But the discovery of Pentecost was that people, in and of themselves, don't have the power to reconcile. Reconciliation is the work of the Spirit.

At Pentecost there was more than reflective listening and acceptance. There was also the proclamation of the prophetic word: "'In the last days,' God says, 'I will pour out my Spirit on all people. Your sons and daughters will prophesy, your young men will see visions, your old men will dream dreams. Even on my servants, both men and women, I will pour out my Spirit in those days, and they will prophesy'" (Acts 2:17-18).

At Pentecost the truth was told. At Pentecost a metanarrative was proclaimed. In times of cultural chaos, the Word is needed.

Even though acceptance of diversity is the popular plea, reconciliation by the Spirit is the only hope for bringing us back from the lostness of our dispersion to a unified culture of love.

The Promise of Pentecost

Modernism was truly a false prophecy. It proclaimed a single language. But the message was not true. It could not fulfill its promises. With the failure of the modernist hope, we have ended up with postmodern confusion. The common message has been deconstructed before our eyes until there is no common thread left to unite people.

But the message of Pentecost calls us back once more. It is a message that you can hear no matter where your scattered experience has taken you. It is a message that is for all and can be heard by all. It is the message of the Spirit.

Middleton and Walsh give us the conclusion: "In our context of cultural confusion, the church needs a prophetic ministry that will 'nurture, nourish, and evoke a consciousness and perception alternative to the consciousness and perception of the dominant culture around us.' Continuing the story is impossible without prophetic discernment that uncovers and dismantles the idolatries of past and present and points forward to a new path of faithful improvisation. Such prophecy is deeply rooted in the biblical story and sheds light on our historical path. In a carnivalesque world of multiple constructions of reality that are put on the market for sale and consumption, a prophetic vision offers the gospel neither as a product nor as for sale. The good news of the gospel, the reopening of the human story, is received as a gift of the sovereign God and offered to all takers for free. And the reception of that gift transforms our reality from a series of postmodern theater pieces or sideshows into the ongoing drama of God's redemption of the world."[4]

As we observed in the first chapter, Paul was not hopeless when it came to a culture with a bad philosophical base like Colossae. Neither can we give up or be discouraged. The plan of Pentecost is still alive. Pentecost calls young men to see visions and old men to dream dreams. It is a call for hope that too many, overwhelmed by the culture, seem to have lost.

The dream of Pentecost envisions a group of loving people who care for each other. Instead of having to have more and more, they seek to give and deny themselves. Instead of trying to get control of the world, they seek to serve the people in it. Instead of comprehending the creation, they seek to know the Creator.

Could this be the end of the preeminence of the Western World? Can you handle it if it is? Can you lose yourself in another dream that is much bigger? Not a myth of progress, but the reality of resurrection.

What the world needs and what we are to be are ultimately the same thing—a Spirit-filled community. The answer can be experienced in a unified community that is based on the truth of Christ—no more, no less.

Questions For Discussion

1. What are some of the signs that you have seen that demonstrate the fall of the modern world?

2. How is the postmodern world more like a carnival than a circus?

3. How could postmodernism be not only the consequence of human arrogance but also the judgment of God?

4. Read Genesis 11:7-8. What were the results of the fall of the Tower of Babel? Describe similar results with the fall of modernism.

5. Read Acts 2:1-21. How are the results of the fall of the Tower of Babel resolved at Pentecost? How can you apply this to postmodernism?

6. What kind of dream should Christians have in the midst of the cultural chaos of postmodernism?

7. What would a "Spirit-filled community" look like?

Notes

————

Chapter 1

1. Tyron Inbody, "Postmodernism: Intellectual Velcro Dragged Across Culture," *Theology Today* (January 1995), 524.

2. Umberto Eco, *Postscript to The Name of the Rose*, trans. William Weaver (San Diego/New York: Harcourt Brace Jovanovich, 1989), 65.

3. Daniel J. Adams, "Toward a Theological Understanding of Postmodernism" (www.crosscurrents.org/adams.htm).

4. C. S. Lewis, *Miracles* (New York: Macmillan, 1947).

Chapter 2

1. Jim Leffel, "Postmodernism: The 'Spirit of the Age'" (www.crossrds.org/rel-rev2.htm).

2. Ibid.

3. Ibid.

Chapter 3

1. My analysis of the relationship of Heraclitus' logos and postmodernism is indebted to the ideas of Victor Knowles of Peace On Earth Ministries.

Chapter 4

1. Emily Saliers, "Closer To Fine." Indigo Girls (CBS Records, 1989). This relationship of Indigo Girls to postmodern thought is also used by J. Richard Middleton

and Brian J. Walsh in *Truth Is Stranger Than It Used To Be* (Downers Grove: IVP, 1995), 57.

2. Milton Jones, "Who Knows?" *21st Century Christian* (May 1999), 39.

3. David Tao, "Where Will You Be When You Get Where You're Going?" *Rejoice and Sing to the Lord* (Austin: Sweet, 1978), p. 35.

4. Francis Schaeffer, *He Is There and He Is Not Silent* (Wheaton: Tyndale, 1972), 99.

Chapter 5

1. The idea of a biblical Babel juxtaposed with the Babel of modernism is eloquently developed in the exceptional work of J. Richard Middleton and Brian J. Walsh, *Truth Is Stranger Than It Used To Be* (Downers Grove: InterVarsity, 1995). For a much more complex and comprehensive analysis of the birth and death of modernism as seen through Columbus and Babel, read this book. The ideas gleaned from this study certainly molded the thoughts in this chapter.

Chapter 6

1. Jean Francois Lyotard, *The Postmodern Condition: A Report on Knowledge* (Minneapolis: University of Minnesota Press, 1984), xxiv.

2. David Garland, *The NIV Application Commentary: Colossians/Philemon* (Grand Rapids: Zondervan, 1998), 155.

3. J. Richard Middleton and Brian J. Walsh, *Truth Is Stranger Than It Used To Be*, p. 71.

4. Ibid., p. 72.

5. Terry Eagleton, "Awakening From Modernity," *Times Literary Supplement*, February 20,1987.

6. Middleton and Walsh, *Truth Is Stranger Than It Used To Be*, p. 73.

7. Ibid., p. 74.

8. Ibid., p. 77.

9. Walter Truett Anderson, *Reality Isn't What It Used To Be: Theatrical Politics, Ready-to-Wear Religion, Global Myths, Primitive Chic and Other Wonders of the Postmodern World* (San Francisco: Harper and Row, 1990), 154.

Chapter 7

1. David Garland, *Colossians/Philemon*, p. 168.

2. Robert Newton Peck, *A Day No Pigs Would Die* (New York: Alfred A. Knopf, 1972), 56.

Chapter 8

1. Robert N. Nash, Jr., *An 8-Track Church In A CD World* (Macon: Smyth and Helwys, 1997), 47.

2. Ibid., p. 50.

3. David Garland, *Colossians/Philemon,* p. 195.

4. Ibid., p. 196.

5. Robert N. Nash, Jr., *An 8-Track Church,* p. 54.

6. Mike Regele, *Death of the Church* (Grand Rapids: Zondervan, 1995) , 19.

Chapter 9

1. Francis Schaeffer, *How Should We Then Live?* (Old Tappan: Fleming H. Revell, 1976), 109.

2. Ibid., p. 216.

3. Ibid., p. 217.

4. Ibid., p. 180.

Chapter 10

1. Kevin Graham Ford, *Jesus For A New Generation* (Downers Grove: InterVarsity, 1995), 218.

2. Ibid., p. 221.

3. Ibid., p. 225.

4. Robert N. Nash, Jr., *An 8-Track Church,* p. 70.

5. Ibid., p. 69.

Chapter 11

1. Milton Jones, *Discipling: The Multiplying Ministry* (Ft. Worth: Star, 1982), 99.

Chapter 12

1. David Garland, *Colossians/Philemon,* p. 261.

2. Ibid.

Chapter 13

1. Urie Bender, *The Witness* (Scottdale: Herald, 1965).

2. Paul L. Tan, *Signs of the Times* (*Encyclopedia of 7700 Illustrations,* 1990).

3. Thom Ranier, *Closing the Back Door* (Forest, VA: Church Growth Institute, 1998), tape 3.

4. Tom Beaudoin, *Virtual Faith* (San Francisco: Jossey-Bass, 1998), 96.

5. Kevin Graham Ford, *Jesus for a New Generation*, pp. 170-239.

6. Ibid., p. 221.

Chapter 14

1. George Will, *Men At Work* (San Francisco: Harper Perennial Library, 1991), 329.

Chapter 15

1. J. Richard Middleton and Brian J. Walsh, *Truth Is Stranger Than It Used to Be*, p. 42.

2. Ibid., pp. 187-194. Both the concept of Babel's relationship to modernism and the resolution at Pentecost is treated extensively in this book. The ideas on this subject presented here originated with Middleton and Walsh.

3. Quoted by Jeffrey Stout, *Ethics After Babel: The Language of Morals and Their Discontents* (Boston: Beacon, 1988), 2.

4. Middleton and Walsh, *Truth Is Stranger Than It Used to Be*, p. 191.